Testimonial

The Rt Hon David Lammy

Oil Dorado? offers a fascinating take on Guyana... or oil producer. This collection of essays elegantly traverses a complex reality with excitement yet caution. Excitement about the possibility of a former colonised nation – excluded from and exploited by the international economy – becoming the subject of enormous international investment. Caution about the impending threat of climate breakdown and the history of corruption and inequality in oil-dependent nations. This book shows an important willingness to learn historical lessons about how to balance economic development with democratic sustainability. Above all, it is grounded in the commitment to ensure the interests of the Guyanese people are protected.

David Lammy has been the Labour Member of Parliament for Tottenham since 2000. He is currently Shadow Secretary of State for Foreign, Commonwealth and Development Affairs. Born of Guyanese parents he is a frequent visitor to Guyana.

Contents

4

ACKNOWLEDGEMENTS

This is the fifth edition of Oil Dorado. Since 2019 all five editions have utilised the efforts of over 100 authors. Each edition is refreshed by at least ten new contributions, as is this one. I thank all contributors very much for their work for which nobody receives a fee. They do it for the book, for the greater understanding of the oil boom, and for Guyana.

The work of subbing these contributions is onerous and often done close to the wire. I thank Richard Lance Keeble for his work on the previous four editions, and Andrew Beck for his brilliant work on this one.

I thank all my friends, families, and contacts on both sides of the Atlantic for their support and contributions, my parents for my Guianese heritage which awoke my interest in Oil Dorado, and my wife Susan for her eternal patience and born-again interest in the land of my birth.

I leave you, dear readers, to judge the work.

John Mair
Oxford, England
February 2023

THE EDITORS

John Mair was born in the then-British Guiana (to an 'Old Guianese' mother: heritage not age) in 1950. He went to Sacred Heart RC School, in Georgetown. John won the top scholarship in the Common Entrance examination in Guiana in 1961. Then his parents emigrated to the UK. He returns regularly to Guyana. He writes there under the nom de guerre Bill Cotton/Reform. John is the proud owner of a Guyana UK High Commission Award. He attended the LSE, Sussex, and Leeds universities. John has taught journalism at the universities of Coventry, Kent, Northampton, Brunel, Edinburgh Napier, and Guyana and at the Communication University of China. He has edited fifty 'hackademic' volumes over the last twelve years on subjects ranging from trust in television, the health of investigative journalism, reporting the Arab Spring, to three volumes on the Leveson Inquiry. His most recent books have been on Inspector Morse in Oxford, ten Oxford authors, reporting the war in Ukraine, and Boris Johnson's time as UK Prime Minister. He created the Coventry Conversations which attracted 350 media movers and shakers to Coventry University. Most recently, he began the My Jericho (Myjericho.co.uk) series of talks in Oxford. In a previous life, he was an award-winning producer/director for the BBC, ITV and Channel 4, and a secondary school teacher.

Richard Lance Keeble is Professor of Journalism at the University of Lincoln, and Honorary Professor at Liverpool Hope University. He has written and edited 48 books on a wide range of media-related topics. In 2020, Routledge published a collection of his recent essays: on George Orwell, literary journalism, war and peace reporting, and journalists and the secret state under the title Journalism Beyond Orwell. He is emeritus editor of Ethical Space: The International Journal of Communication Ethics which he launched in 2003, and joint editor of George Orwell Studies. From 2013 to 2020 he was chair of the Orwell Society. In 2011, he gained a National Teaching Fellowship, the highest award for teachers in higher education in the U.K., and in 2014 he was given a Lifetime Achievement Award by the Association for Journalism Education. He is a member of Louth

Male Voice Choir, Louth Film Club, and (through thick and thin) Nottinghamshire County Cricket Club.

Andrew Beck worked in UK secondary, further, and higher education for forty-two years, lastly as International Partnership Manager for Coventry University's Faculty of Arts and Humanities. He is author of best-selling and oft cited works such as Cultural Work and Communication Studies: The Essential Introduction, as well as having served as chief examiner for public and professional examinations. Retired from full-time work he continues to teach at and advise international universities, as well as researching and publishing on a range of media issues. Recent publications include contributions to books on Covid-19, the Ukraine war, Boris Johnson's premiership, as well as occasional features for China Eye.

Oil

John Agard

Gushing from earth's abundance
a dream of black gold

to eel your way through fingers
coaxing a glow out of skin

or simply playing your role
of a sizzling puddle in a pan.

A little of you, says the hymn,
will keep a lamp burning

till the break of day. Sing
hosanna sing.

Yet, the ever slick one,
you anoint a prophet's brow

as well as the wheels of war.
Oil, whose side are you on?

About the contributor

John Agard, born and educated in Georgetown, Guyana, is the author of many books for both adult and young readers. He was awarded the Casa de las Americas Poetry Prize for Man To Pan, his collection of poems inspired by the evolution of the steel pan. Twice winner of the Guyana Prize, he was BBC poet-in-residence in 1998 and received the Queen's Gold Medal for Poetry in 2012.

PRELUDE: OIL AND EL DORADO - THE MYTHS

Chapter One

Sir Walter Raleigh and El Dorado: The myth traced to source

For more than 500 years the quest for El Dorado, the mythical city of gold in South America, has persisted. Nobody has ever found it, not even the original explorer Sir Walter Raleigh. Christopher Minster explores the background

El Dorado, the legendary lost city of gold rumoured to be somewhere in the unexplored interior of South America, claimed many victims as thousands of Europeans braved flooded rivers, frosty highlands, endless plains, and steamy jungles in the vain search for gold.

However, the most well known of the obsessed men who searched for it must be Sir Walter Raleigh, the legendary Elizabethan courtier who made two trips to South America to search for it.

The myth itself

There is a grain of truth in the El Dorado myth. The Muisca culture of Colombia had a tradition where their king would cover himself in gold dust and dive into Lake Guatavitá. Raleigh heard the story and began searchingfor the kingdom of El Dorado, 'the Gilded One'.

Lake Guatavitá was dredged and some gold was found, but not very much, so the legend persisted. The supposed location of the lost city changed frequently as dozens of expeditions failed to find it. By 1580 or so, the lost city of gold was thought to be in the mountains of present-day Guyana, a harsh and inaccessible place. The city of gold was referred to as El Dorado or Manoa, after a city told of by a Spaniard who had been held captive by natives for ten years.

Sir Walter arrives

Sir Walter Raleigh was a member of the court of Queen Elizabeth I of England, whose favour he enjoyed. He was a true Renaissance man: he wrote history and poetry, was a decorated sailor, and dedicated explorer and settler. He fell out of favour with the Queen when he secretly married one of her maids in 1592. He was even imprisoned in the Tower of London for a time.

However, he talked his way out of the Tower and convinced the Queen to allow him to mount an expedition to the New World to conquer El Dorado before the Spanish found it. Never one to miss the chance to outdo the Spanish, the Queen agreed to send Raleigh on his quest.

The capture of Trinidad

Raleigh and his brother Sir John Gilbert rounded up investors, soldiers, ships, and supplies. On 6 February 1595, they set out from England with five small ships. His expedition was an act of open hostility against Spain, which jealously guarded its New World possessions.

They reached Trinidad where they cautiously checked out the Spanish forces. The Englishmen attacked and captured the town of San Jose. They took an important prisoner on the raid, Antonio de Berrío, a high-ranking Spaniard who had spent years searching for El Dorado himself. Berrío told Raleigh what he knew about Manoa and El Dorado, trying to discourage theEnglishman from continuing his quest, but his warnings were in vain.

Raleigh left his ships anchored at Trinidad and took only 100 men to the mainland to begin his search. His plan was to go up the Orinoco River to the Caroni River and then follow it until he reached a legendary lake where he would find the city of Manoa. Raleigh had caught wind of a massive Spanish expedition to the area, so he was in a hurry to get under way.

He and his men headed up the Orinoco on a collection of rafts, ships, boats, and even a modified galley. Although they were aided by natives who knew the river, the going was very tough as they had to fight the current of the mighty Orinoco River. The men, a collection of desperate sailors and cut-throats from England, were unruly and difficult to manage.

Topiawari

Laboriously Raleigh and his men made their way upriver. They found a friendly village, ruled by an aged chieftain named Topiawari. As he had been doing since arriving on the continent, Raleigh made friends by announcing that he was an enemy of the Spanish, who were widely detested by the natives. Topiawari told Raleigh of a rich culture living in the mountains. Raleigh easily convinced himself that the culture was an offshoot of the rich Inca culture of Peru and that it must be the fabled city of Manoa. The Spanish set out up the Caroni River, sending out scouts to look for gold and mines, all the while making friends with any natives they encountered. His scouts brought back rocks, hoping that further analysis would reveal gold ore.

Although Raleigh thought he was close, he decided to turn around. The rains were increasing, making the rivers even more treacherous, and he also feared being caught by the rumoured Spanish expedition. He felt he had enough evidence with his rock samples to drum up enthusiasm back in England for a return venture. He made an alliance with Topiawari, promising mutual aid when he returned. The English would help fight the Spanish, and the natives would help Raleigh find and conquer Manoa. As part of the deal, Raleigh left two men behind and took Topiawari's son back to England. As they were travelling downstream the return journey was much easier. The Englishmen were joyful at seeing their ships still anchored off Trinidad.

Return to England

Raleigh paused on his way back to England for a bit of privateering, attacking the island of Margarita and then the port of Cumaná, where he dropped off Berrío, who had remained a prisoner on board Raleigh's ships while he looked for Manoa. Raleigh returned to England in August 1595 and was disappointed to learn that news of his expedition had preceded him andthat it was already considered a failure.

Queen Elizabeth had little interest in the rocks he brought back. His enemies seized upon his journey as an opportunity to slander him, claiming that the rocks were either fake or worthless. Raleigh defended himself ably but was surprised to find very little enthusiasm in his home country for a return trip to Guiana.

The legacy of Raleigh's first search for El Dorado

Raleigh would get his return trip to Guiana, but not until 1617, more than 20years later. This second journey was a complete failure and led directly to Raleigh's execution back in England.

In between, Raleigh financed and supported other English expeditions to Guiana, which brought him more 'proof', but the search for El Dorado was becoming a hard sell.

In 1617, he returned to the New World on a second expedition, this time with Lawrence Kemys and his son, Watt Raleigh, to continue his quest for El Dorado. However, Raleigh, by now an old man, stayed behind in a camp onthe island of Trinidad. Watt Raleigh was killed in a battle with Spaniards and Kemys subsequently committed suicide. Upon Raleigh's return toEngland, King James ordered him to be beheaded for disobeying orders to avoid conflict with the Spanish. He was executed in 1618.

Raleigh's greatest accomplishment may have been in creating good relations between the English and the natives of South America. Although Topiawari passed away not long after Raleigh's first voyage, the goodwill remained, and future English explorers benefitted from it.

Today, Sir Walter Raleigh is remembered for many things, including his writings and his participation in the 1596 attack on the Spanish port of Cadiz, but he will forever be associated with the vain quest for El Dorado.

Reference

Robert Silverberg (1985) The Golden Dream: Seekers of El Dorado, Athens: Ohio University Press.

About the contributor

Christopher Minster is a Professor at the Universidad San Francisco de Quitoin Ecuador. He is a specialist in Latin American literature and history with a PhD in Spanish from Ohio State University.

Chapter Two

The oil baccoo takes up residence

In a piece written in 2019 Indranie Deolall recalls a cautionary Guyanese folktale in which fragile receptacles, waiting to be freed by the unsuspecting, conceal dangerous abilities and unquenchable appetites. Is this a warning for the years ahead?

As a child I loved accompanying my stout father, Mr Big, to the city sea wall for his regular swim after a brisk walk atop the crumbling Fort Groyne. Built near the strategic site of a former British garrison that watched over the coveted sliver of low-lying coastline and the adjoining mouth of the Demerara River, the concrete erosion barrier jutted out into the ocean like a fat index finger, at the far end of breezy Kingston.

It was here, in 1781, that British Lieutenant Colonel Robert Kingston decided to establish the little settlement that would become the capital Georgetown, after capturing the Dutch colony of Demerara-Essequibo and moving the administrative centre from Borselen Island far up the murky waterway.

While Dad waded out, past the squelchy flats, to exercise in the deeper waters discoloured grey-brown by Amazonian mud, I danced barefoot on the warm beach, and screamed and squinted at him, a mere dot, bouncing up and down in the waves.

Racing in the surf, hair streaming, the sharp taste of salt in my mouth, I would search for signs of that history, specimens and sea glass gems worn smooth by the frothing Atlantic that has witnessed centuries of conflict and ships ferrying foreign explorers forever fixed on finding fame and fortune.

One evening, intrigued by the Portuguese man-o-war that drifted in with the currents, I bent to pick up the purple and blue blob, when my family, who had accompanied us, screamed at me in a chorus to drop it. Instead, I collected the tiny, coloured bottles scattered among the detritus, as the light faded. But these were all hurled away by my strangely angry mother. I learnt, to my chagrin and shock, that like 'the floating terror', no corked glass container, regardless of how pretty the hue, was to be even touched, and God forbid, retained and opened.

Our cautionary folktales, such as those she related that night, warn of the temperamental forces that supposedly lie trapped in fragile receptacles waiting to be freed by the unsuspecting, their size concealing dangerous abilities and unquenchable appetites.

The origins of baccoo

Of West African origin, according to the late Guyanese linguist and lexicographer, Dr Richard Allsopp, the word baccoo stems from ba-ku meaning death/corpse and led to the Saramaccan bakulu, a dwarf-spirit.

According to the Creole expert in the Dictionary of Caribbean English Usage, the baccoo is 'an active, wicked spirit believed to take the form of some small, living, partly human being that must be kept in a bottle and may be commanded either to bring its owner great wealth or to do harm to other persons'.

With an unexplained lust for the plump bacuba or red-skinned bananas belonging to the Cavendish group, and fresh milk, the creature often misbehaves by abruptly moving items, pelting homes with rocks, and causing general mayhem.

Suspicious displays of excess gold and sudden riches are put down to a well-fed baccoo but since they tend to be mischievous, intelligent and deceitful, the infernal beings shapeshift, tormenting and destroying their owners when the mood, madness, and hunger strike.

The oil baccoo is out

These days, besides the usual abundant catch of prawns and fish, local seas are finally yielding deep-down troves of treasures tens of millions of years old, that could bring unimagined wealth to an unprepared nation, one of the most impoverished in the hemisphere.

The oil baccoo is out. Mr Big, in this case, is the savvy pack leader, the Texas-based giant ExxonMobil (XOM), among the world's largest publicly traded international energy companies, which is pinning its hopes on Guyana for a revival.

The firm's astonishing exploration success in just the last few years has made the Guyana basin an exciting Oil Dorado, pulling the most prominent firms in the industry to snap up prime acreage. In May 2015, the XOM-led consortium announced its first 'significant' find after a decades-long search with the Liza-1 well in the lucrative and huge 6.6m. acre Stabroek Block, yielding high-quality oil-bearing sandstone reservoirs, about 120 miles offshore Crude prices were plummeting at the time, sinking to a 12-year low of about US $26 a barrel in 2016.

Foreign ownership

ExxonMobil's Esso Exploration and Production Guyana Ltd holds a 45 per cent stake in the block. The subsidiary of another major American corporation, Hess Guyana Exploration, controls 30 per cent. China's National Offshore Oil Corporation (CNOOC), which, in January 2019, closed its milestone US$15.1bn acquisition of Canadian Nexen, owns 25 per cent through its re-branded CNOOC International division.

Since then, the discoveries keep coming. Just this year, XOM announced its eleventh and twelfth major oil and gas finds in the south-eastern section, Tilapia-1 and Haimara-1, bearing the common names of local fishes, and taking its Guyana estimated recoverable resources to more than five billion barrels of oil equivalent.

With the country's first oil well expected to have produced up to 120,000 barrels per day by early 2020, and at least another dozen or so likely, some analysts predict production could exceed a million barrels daily over the next decade, rocketing this small country from a nobody to a new-found star shining in the Organisation of Petroleum Exporting Countries' (OPEC) top ten. A mere two of the wildcat wells have missed, representing a phenomenalsuccess rate of more than 90 per cent.

Given its population of about 800,000, a large diaspora, and a meagre Gross Domestic Product (GDP) per capita of just over US$4,000, Guyana stands on the brink of unprecedented riches.

However, it will need to set aside long simmering ethnic mistrust and endless party bickering, heightened by the recent surprise passage of a divisive no confidence motion in the government, and get its act together before the non-renewable oil runs outs. Avoiding the 'resource curse' that so visibly haunts states like oil bulwark Venezuela, imploding next door, and aggressively renewing claims to three quarters of Guyana, will mean disciplined investing in a substantial sovereign wealth fund.

Even with the low 2 per cent royalty on gross earnings and 50 per cent of oil proceeds, at the current average market price of $50 per barrel, Guyana can expect to earn US$1m. a day.

Realms of gold

Simon Flowers, chairman and chief analyst of respected Scotland-based global resources research and consultancy group Wood Mackenzie, has spoken of his sense of wonder over Guyana. Rephrasing the famous lines of Romantic poet John Keats' 'On First Looking into Chapman's Homer', he posted: 'I felt like some watcher of the skies when a new planet swims into his ken.' Incidentally, the poem starts with the phrase: 'Much have I travell'd in the realms of gold'.

In an online piece Flowers acknowledged 'The discovery of a major new oil player like Guyana instils the same sense dwonder on we oil industry devotees. Few oil-producing countries produce more than one million barrels per day. Outside of OPEC, you can count them on two hands: Canada, USAand Mexico, UK and Norway, China, Brazil and Oman, Russia and most recently Kazakhstan – the only new member in the 21st century. New admissions to the group don't happen very often. Guyana, with no upstream oil industry four years ago, has a very good chance of joining this elite group.'

In a February 2019 commentary on what Guyana can learn from the Venezuelan crisis (see chapter 24 of this book), he warned against the temptation 'to spend, spend, spend'. Opposing dependence on a single source of revenue, Flowers singled out infrastructure building and raising education standards to help develop other sectors: 'Our analysis of the upstream project assumes total investment of over $30bn, plateauing at $5bn annually in the early 2020s as the known discoveries are developed; all perhaps matched by investment down the value chain onshore. Tax revenues kick in from the mid-2020s and build up quickly to more than $10bn per annum.'

Flowers pointed out: 'For such a small economy, the scale of development is staggering. Assuming oil production of one million barrels daily by 2030,Guyana's output per person will be higher than any other major oil producer. A four-fold increase in the size of its economy over a decade is possible, catapulting Guyana into the high-income bracket.'

And he stressed: 'It will be a delicate balancing act. The role of government is also central to success in setting clear energy policy, establishing firm and independent regulation, and a stable fiscal policy. These set a framework for close collaboration with international operators. The fate of Venezuela is all the incentive needed to get this right.'

A fairy tale

Exxon's senior vice-president Neil Chapman, a management board member, compared the Guyana developments to the magic of a 'fairy tale' at the company's analysts' day in March 2018. According to the 2012 World Petroleum Resources Project by the United States Geological Survey, the assessed provinces of the region including South America and the Caribbean have a mean estimate of 12.6bn barrels of oil in offshore reservoirs. The Guyana Suriname Basin has at least 12bn barrels.

As the baccoos remind us, it is painfully ironic that the very resources slated to bring Guyana unexpected wealth will also contribute to increasing vulnerability. Most experts agree the burning of non-renewable fossil fuels such as oil and natural gas releases carbon dioxide into the atmosphere, thickening the layers of greenhouse gases and making the earth warmer.

This could mean a rather grim future for low-lying and impoverished countries like Guyana, with the bulk of the population and industries confined to a fragile and narrow strip of coastland. Residents already struggle with the regular consequences of floods with each black sky and heavy rainfall, rising sea levels and weather shifts. The worst-case context would mean eventually relocating the entire belt to higher zones further inland. Declining to hear oil giant ExxonMobil's appeal in its suit with the state of Massachusetts, in January 2019 the United States Supreme Court issued an important ruling for ongoing legal battles around climate change. In the appeal, XOM tried to block the release of incriminating records that it knew burning fossil fuels alters the climate. Massachusetts attorney general Maura Hayley filed the suit against the giant in 2016 alleging that it violated state consumer protection rules and misled investors about the impact of fossil fuels on climate change, and the ensuing business risks, media reports indicated.

American journalist Steve Coll describes an illuminating exchange in 2001 between then President George W. Bush and the Indian Prime Minister Atal Bihari Vajpayee. Worried that ExxonMobil was delaying a deal with India's largest state-owned oil company, Vajpayee allegedly asked Bush: 'Why don't you just tell them what to do?' The 43rd President's response was ominous: 'Nobody tells those guys what to do!' Much like the rampaging Guyanese baccoos.

About the contributor

Indranie Deolall is a Guyanese-born journalist based in Trinidad. She is a columnist for the private newspaper Stabroek News.

SECTION 1: SETTING THE GUYANA SCENE IN 2023

Big oil, big issues

John Mair

Every Man, Woman and Child in British Guiana Must Become Oil-Minded!

> - The Daily Chronicle, British-Guiana,
> Tuesday 18 November 1932

This book is a labour of love: a festschrift to my mother's land and that of her mothers, her grandmothers, and great grandmothers before her for two centuries. They have historical form.

I was born in the then-British Guiana to an 'old Guianese' family. I go back 'home' frequently, and have seen it develop from an impoverished state, second only to Haiti in heavily indebted poor country (HIPC) terms, brains drained to the US, Canada, and the U.K., through its false rebirth as a narco-economy trans-shipping 'whitegold' cocaine from Colombia to the US and Europe, through the long, slow death of the sugar industry (in which I was brought up), to the new light at the end of the tunnel: a huge booming oil economy, Oil Dorado.

A very brief history of oil and Guyana

The potential for oil in Guyana was recognised by Dutch explorers in the 1700s and the first onshore exploration wells were drilled in 1916. There was little offshore oil exploration interest until the late 1960s. This was followed by a period of considerable activity in the 1970s when twenty-two wells were drilled. Disappointingly, no offshore commercial discoveries resulted from this activity.

However, Guyana's fortunes changed in 2015 with the Liza discovery, 120 miles off the coast of Guyana in deep water of some

5,719 feet, in the Stabroek Block. Since then, history has accelerated at pace. Today, Guyana is the world's new oil frontier.

The Guyana oil fields in January 2023

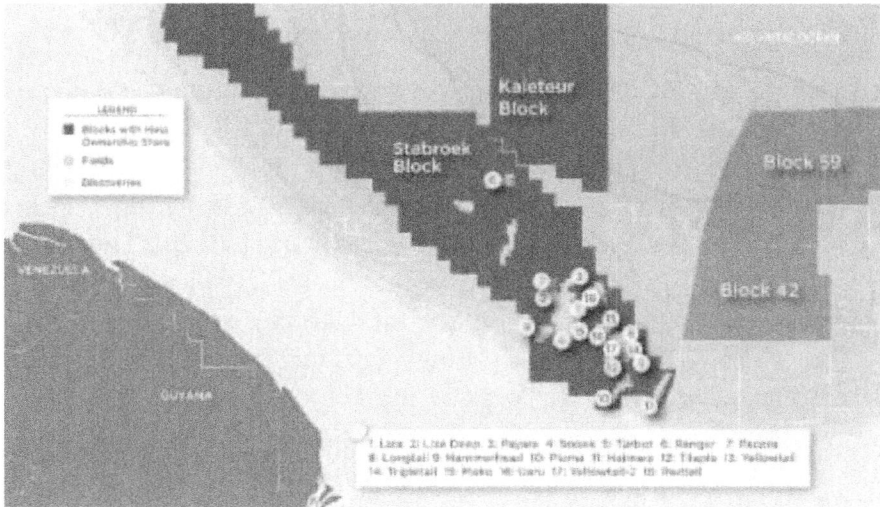

Source: Hess

Is Oil Dorado now a reality?

Four years ago, in the first edition of this book, calling Guyana 'Oil Dorado' may have verged on hype; today it is a massive understatement. Guyana is the Klondike of the Oil World. Countries from India to China to Saudi and the UAE are coming calling. The multi-national oil majors from across the world are fighting to get a share of the action there or in Suriname. In the jargon of the industry, they are 'in play' or even are 'big plays'. Oil men talk of Guyana as the most exciting prospect, one of their most successful finds for years.

The figures involved are quite unprecedented and simply staggering. Billions of barrels of oil are found with ease. To date, ExxonMobil and their partners have successfully drilled 33 wells in the Stabroek block alone. Their hit rate of good to bad wells, wet to dry, is not far off 90 per cent, where the industry average is 20 per cent at best.

Exxon estimates 11.2m barrels of oil in just that field. That is nearly a third of the world's discoveries of oil in the last five years. Guyana has gone from nowhere to number seventeen in the world chart of oil reserves.

The oil just keeps flowing offshore Guyana

'First oil' was lifted in December 2019; that was just four years after its first being discovered, and a near record for Big Oil. Today it is pumped out and refined in two Floating Production Storage and Offloading vessels (FPSOs) Liza 1 and Liza Unity, currently extracting 344,000 barrels of oil per day for sale on the world market. In 2022, nearly 50 per cent of Guyana's black gold went to oil-hungry Europe suffering energy shortages due to the war in Ukraine. One more FPSO, Prosperity, is being built in Singapore and on the way. Ten are expected to be operating at 'peak oil' in 2027.

In essence, these FPSOs are floating mini oil refineries pumping oil and gas from wells nearly 6000ft below the Atlantic Ocean. These fuels are then separated from the mud, which is pumped back in or sent ashore. At the moment, so too is most of the gas. Some of that is flared. Some will be sent ashore once the pipeline to shore is set up and running. The light sweet high-quality (important) Brent crude is then tankered off to the world market. It is much sought after. In January 2023 Prime Minister Modi of India proposed a long-range deal to Guyana's President Alfori for buying Guyana's oil wholesale.

In 2022 there were 94 lifts, of which 13 went to the government of Guyana, and 81 went to the oil stakeholding companies. The government gets thirteen million barrels to be auctioned off by them at the current world price of US$89 per barrel. That means a revenue of not far off $100m per lift, over $1bn to the government in total in 2022. In August 2022 the Inter-American Development Bank (IDB) reported that 60 per cent of Guyana's GDP in 2022 would come from oil. In any case Guyana's GDP is already up 47.5 per cent in that year.

In the first half of 2022 the Guyana oil industry grew by 75 per cent. Virtually every other month new discoveries in Stabroek block are announced. This has been one of the most prolific exploration blocks of all time. If measured on exploration success rate, it probably does not have an equivalent in the world. In 2022 alone, ExxonMobil announced four new discoveries, taking their total number of working wells to 33.

Much of the 'profit oil' goes to ExxonMobil and partners; that's 81 lifts, worth $8bn in 2022. The Guyana Natural Resources Fund, the country's sovereign wealth fund, had reserves of $1.27bn at the end of 2022. That fund is regularly raided by the government, perfectly legally, for public spending. There is now in place a supervisory board for the NRF headed by the impeccable Brigadier General (retired) Joe Singh.

The Stabroek Field offshore Guyana: Discoveries to December 2021

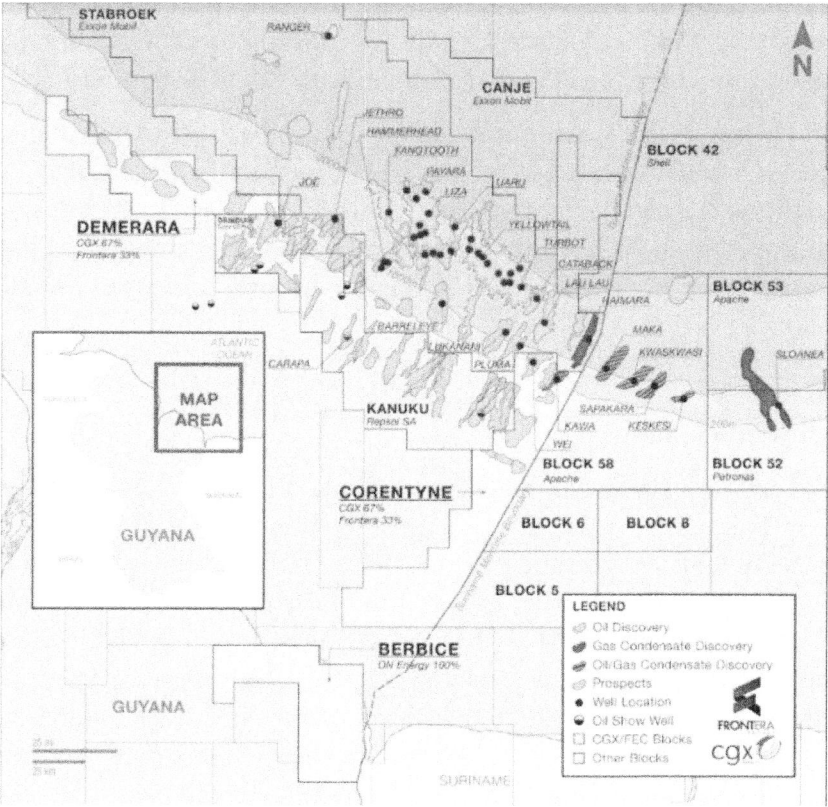

Source: CGX

How much oil is there?

The oil-rich Stabroek Block is 6.6 million acres (26,800 square kilometres) in size. ExxonMobil, through its subsidiary Esso Exploration and Production Guyana Limited (EEPGL), is the operator and holds a 45 per cent interest in the block. Hess Guyana Exploration Ltd holds a 30 per cent interest, and China National Offshore Oil Corporation (CNOOC) Petroleum Guyana Limited, a wholly owned subsidiary of CNOOC Limited, holds 25 per cent.

Stabroek is just one block. There are eight others offshore Guyana, of which five are actively being explored. And then there is Suriname too. Back in 2012, the United States Geological Survey estimated there were 13.6bn barrels of oil and 32 trillion cubic feet of natural gas yet to be discovered in the Guyana Suriname Basin. That ceiling has nearly been reached already. ExxonMobil recently estimated there could be up to 20bn barrels of oil equivalent in that Basin.

In December 2021, Americas Market Intelligence estimated that by 2035 Guyana could easily be the biggest per-capita producer of oil in the world, producing 1.4m barrels per day. In 2022, Rystad Energy said they would be producing more oil offshore than the US by that date. The figures are dreamlike for a Third World country, especially a former HIPC.

How much money?

Oil quantities are beyond belief, as are oil riches. But, sadly, there are not too many riches for the host country. In 2016 the then-government of Guyana negotiated a very lopsided Production Sharing Agreement with ExxonMobil. The oil minister at the time, Raphael Trotman, was ill advised and simply did not accept professional opinion. Guyana now gets only2 per cent of net royalties from oil. Many commentators argue that this is way below the going market world rate. Costs are also front-loaded to take in those of exploration pre 'first oil'. So far, according to ExxonMobil, just that one company's total investments in Guyana amounts to $62bn. The cake is divided up so that Guyana gets but a small slice. Whether that 2016 contract can or will be re-negotiated forms the basis of much legal and political argument in and out of Guyana.

How profitable is Guyana oil?

In July 2022, Norwegian research company Rystad Energy estimated the value of the Stabroek block alone to be US$41bn.

'First oil' from the Liza Phase 1 development flowed on 20 December 2019, which was subsequently named National Petroleum Day in Guyana. The Liza 1 floating production, storage, and offloading vessel (FPSO) is designed to produce up to 120,000 barrels per day. The first 1m barrels of oil were lifted and exported by tanker on 20 January 2020. The Liza Phase 2 development came on stream in mid-2022 using the Liza Unity FPSO. That was designed to produce 220,000 barrels per day. And it is doing just that.

The nearby Payara development has its 'first oil' planned for 2023 utilising the Prosperity FPSO which was also designed to produce 220,000 barrels per day.The current oil discoveries will be produced from at least five FPSOs and it is estimated that Guyana could be producing more than 1m barrels per day by 2027 after the development of Yellowtail. This means that Guyana will produce more oil per capita than Kuwait.

In January 2023 the government of Guyana invited expressions of interest in fourteen new offshore blocks, eleven in shallow water, three in the deep sea area. Wood MacKenzie estimates there could be up to 25bn barrels in those blocks. The Petroleum Production Sharing Agreement (PSA) contracts for these will be much more favourable to Guyana as a country than the 2016 ExxonMobil one. They have to be.

In 2016, the year following the first discovery, the world oil price (Brent) hit a low of US$25 per barrel. On 20 January 2023 the price of oil was US$86 per barrel. Liza Phase 1, 2, and Payara development break-evens are priced at US$35 and US$25 per barrel. So the Guyana oilfields are not just plentiful but incredibly profitable.

Oil Dorado's effect on the economy, the ordinary citizen

On Monday, 16 January 2023, the Senior Minister in the Office of the President with responsibility for Finance, Dr Ashni Singh presented the National Budget for 2023. Total government spending was GY$782billion (US$3.75 billion), up 41 per cent on 2022. There will be no new taxes but there will be investment in infrastructure. Of government revenue, nearly 30 per cent will come from oil. Guyana's economy grew by 61 per cent in 2022, and is expected to grow by a further 25 per cent in 2023. Trickle-down economics and the multiplier effect means that some of that spending will percolate down to the citizen in the street. Hopefully.

From widescreen to closeup

That's the big Guyana picture. Now it's time for some detailed analysis. The first section of this edition consists entirely of new contributions to the debate. It attempts to tackle the big issues facing Oil Dorado today and maybe offer some solutions.

First in to bat the indomitable Dr Tulsi Dyal Singh, Berbice-born but now lost in the badlands of Midland, Texas. He gave up medicine for investing in and chairing a bank in the Permian Basin. Tulsi observes his mother's land from afar and with regular visits. In 'Guyana enters fourth year producing oil: the future is bright!' he looks at future oil auctions offshore Guyana and concludes, 'I believe that Guyana's premium oil, cheap to extract and close to major markets will be in great demand even when fossil fuel becomes second to renewable sources of energy, as will happen over the next two decades'.

The company CGX should be the bright shining star of the oil boom in Guyana. It was first into the field two and more decades ago. Now it is not. The CGX star is now barely glistening. Why? In 'All that glisters is not gold: The CGX story' I examine the sad history of the company which, rather than growing in size, seems to be losing limbs regularly à la Monty Python. Early 2023 is crunch time for CGX with the exploration of their Wei-1 well. It's make or break. At long last there is some revenue for the company who have taken over most of CGX's assets. I conclude, 'The future onshore is not bright. Offshore there is a little more hope'.

Geoffrey Da Silva is an insider turned outsider. He was a minister in a previous PPP government and then Guyana's ambassador to Venezuela from 2011 to 2015. There he was in an ideal position to observe the resource curse and the effect on one country. In 'One Guyana" he looks at the promise and performance of his party's new government 'One Guyana' policy and advises, 'The overwhelming majority of Guyanese want a people's 'Oil Dorado' where there are equal opportunities so that not one individual or family is left behind. The priority must be to ensure that all workers, farmers, the unemployed, the marginalized, the poor and the hungry will enjoy higher income levels, improved social services, and better living standards.'

Dr Riyad Insanally has been at the epicentre of Guyana diplomacy for three decades. He was Ambassador to the USA from 2016 to 2021 when the first big oil deals were being done. To an extent, sadly, he was an outsider on them. Then oil minister Rafael Trotman negotiated directly near solo with Exxon Mobil. In 'The Venezuela border controversy: Diplomacy must continue to complement the ICJ process' Ambassador Insanally examines the biggest diplomatic headache facing Guyana today (as it has done for 125 years): its neighbour's claim to one-third of its land mass in Essequibo and the offshore riches there. He says that Guyana's defence has to be twin-track -- legal in the ICJ, plus the normal diplomatic channels. He argues that, 'Guyana's narrative has to be continuously and forcefully repeated at every possible opportunity, as an overriding foreign policy imperative'.

China has a legitimate business interest in the future of Oil Dorado. CNOOC, their national oil corporation, has had a 25 per cent stake in the prolific Stabroek Field almost from the beginning. Why? Jungi Yan and Ali Hasan Humza from the Communication University of China in Beijing examine the mutual interest of the two countries in

'Why is China interested in Guyana's oil?' And, not surprisingly, they conclude that it is good for both of them: 'China has a great demand for energy, minerals, and strong infrastructure capacity, which are complementary to the economic development of Guyana'. Professor Anthony Bryan is the doyen of Caribbean oil academics at UWI and the University of Miami. He has written in every edition of Oil Dorado. In his essay 'Getting from here to there: Guyana's Oil Dorado journey' he warns, 'Guyana could become one of the world's richest nations per capita but managing public expectations is critical, or a crisis of expectations can have a negative impact on the country's ability to meet its goals'.

Real estate prices are going through the roof in Guyana. So too the prices of spare sugar estate land like the Houston Plantation slap bang in Shorebase Central on the East Bank Demerara. Just 500 acres left for one family but worth a king's ramson to the Vieiras. I look at the history and the prognosis for this piece of land gold. In my view, 'What happens to that last 500 acres of those former sugar cane fields is a portent for Guyana's future. Sugar is dead, oil is alive. It is unlikely that the Vieira dynasty will lose out'.

Dr Melissa Varswyk is the CEO of the Georgetown American University, Guyana. In 'On the brighter side of Oil Dorado' she looks on the good side of the oil boom. She heads Women in Energy and pleads, 'Let us cooperate for Guyana. Let us cooperate for our land. Let us resolve to fight together. See, we do it right together. Can we do it? Yes, we can!'

Still in the world of the Caribbean academia, Dr Lorraine Sobers of UWI is the female counterpart to Anthony Bryan. The doyenne. Her original interest is scientific. In 'Footing the bill for climate change with petrodollars' Dr Sobers concludes, 'Guyana holds a unique position being a long-standing significant carbon sink, swiftly becoming a significant oil producer, and now set to rapidly transition to cleaner energy while developing a poor nation in less than a decade. The country will need every petrodollar it earns to face the future'.

Then we turn to the effect of Oil Dorado on the ordinary man or woman in the Guyanese street. Narissa Dookeran is a blogger, sometime teacher, and real consumer. Hers is the view from the bottom up. In 'Will oil wealth trickle down to benefit ordinary Guyanese?' she dreams it will: 'With good governance and management of state resources Guyana can truly be Oil Dorado!'

Finally, we offer a look at Guyana's oil boom from the perspective of Trinidad and Tobago. Mark Wilson examines Guyana's January 2023 budget with an eye to both the economic and climate ramifications of Oil Dorado.

Guyana's oil boom brings great wealth but it also brings many problems. Read on.

Chapter Three

Guyana enters fourth year producing oil: the future is bright!

Guyana has successfully negotiated its toddler years in the oil and gas business. As it enters its fourth year as an oil producer and exporter, Dr Tulsi Dyal Singh explains how opportunities abound to transform the nation into a model of success

The first three years of Guyana's immersion in the business of oil and gas has seen a steady ramping up of production by the main operator ExxonMobil and its subcontractors. First, Liza Destiny came online in December 2019, but it suffered major operational setbacks lasting several months. Those have been resolved and it is now running well ahead of its rated capacity of 120,000 barrels at 140,000 barrels of oil per day. Then the much larger Liza Unity came on stream in April 2022, and is now producing at full capacity of 220,000 barrels per day. Going into 2023, total production from these two platforms is expected to continue at 360,000 barrels per day, then increase dramatically when the Payara platform, rated at 220,000 barrels per day, kicks in later this year. Hess Corp, the most vocal of the oil giants in the triumvirate that owns the rights to the Stabroek block, projects a production rate of 1.2m barrels per day in 2027.

There is money in the bank

By the end of 2022, Guyana had earned around nineteen million barrels of oil as its profit share, in addition to its royalty of two per cent on all oil sold by operators. At the end of 2022 the balance in the nation's Natural Resource Fund (NRF), the Sovereign Wealth Fund, was US$1.26bn.

The Bank of Guyana's financial statement on the NRF shows that there were two withdrawals of US$200m each in 2022 to the nation's Consolidated Fund. The amount available for withdrawal each year is dependent on the amount of money that was deposited in the NRF the previous calendar year. It is explicitly quantified using a sliding scale incorporated in the NRF Act of 2021, under the First Schedule titled 'Calculating the Ceiling on Annual Withdrawal'. Just over US$1.25bn entered the NRF in 2022.

By applying the First Schedule mentioned above, that income allows the government to withdraw about US$1bn into the Consolidated Fund for use in 2023. That would be a massive boost to the income side of the 2023 national budget. For reference, Guyana's budgeted current revenues from all sources, excluding oil, for 2022 was less than US$1.5bn. What a difference a year makes!

Reserves keep climbing

ExxonMobil continues to make new oil discoveries. Nine new finds were announced by Exxon in the course of 2022. At mid-year, Exxon confirmed that Guyana's recoverable reserves were eleven billion barrels of oil equivalent. Since then, four new finds have been announced: Seabob 1; Kiru-Kiru 1; Sailfin 1; and Yarrow 1. These would surely increase the recoverable reserves when Exxon updates their estimates. How high will it go?

There are many more drill sites within Exxon's Stabroek Block. Besides, other operators are intensifying their exploration in adjacent and nearby blocks. How high can it go?

Twenty-eight new blocks coming up for auction

The Government of Guyana is planning to auction 28 new blocks offshore later this year. These new blocks collectively amount to seven million acres. Vice President Bharrat Jagdeo, the de facto oil supremo, has announced plans for a revamped set of auction criteria aimed at removing the grave inequities in the 2016 Petroleum Agreement between Guyana and ExxonMobil in the Stabroek block, as well as obtaining better terms for Guyana, in particular aiming for Guyana to receive more money up front, in the life cycle of production from these oil blocks. These criteria include: winning bidders paying Guyana competitive signing bonuses; paying corporate income taxes on their profits; higher royalties; and higher up-front profit-sharing for Guyana by pushing the operators' cost recovery schedules further back in the life cycle of each block. Of course, money from these new blocks, if any become productive, would still be a few years off.

Premium rocks are yielding premium oil and earning premium prices

Guyana's oil is rated as 'light and sweet', the kind that is easier to refine, and yields higher proportions of premium products and lower amounts of pollutants. Guyana benefits by an extra US$5 per barrel currently for this high-quality crude oil versus the other widely traded grades of oil. It seems also that the native sandstone rocks hosting Guyana's oil are highly porous, allowing for the drill bits to crunch their way to the oil, speeding up drilling time and reducing drilling expenses. This is a bonanza in itself.

The associated gas will be monetised

Since the start of oil production, the associated gas that comes up with the oil has been used to power some of the functions of the Floating Production, Storage and Offloading (FPSO) platforms. Initially, the associated gas was reinjected into the host rock to aid production but technical problems with reinjection forced the operators to flare the excess gas. A better solution is in sight. A large portion of the gas, 50 million cubic feet per day initially, will be transported by pipeline to Guyana's shore, to generate 300 Megawatts of electricity for the country. The electricity supply in Guyana has historically been inefficient, expensive, unreliable, and polluting. The high cost of electricity has stymied basic manufacturing. Cheaper power will help make Guyanese entrepreneurs competitive in the market for manufactured products, including natural gas based agricultural fertilizers, not to mention eliminating the incessant blackouts that have chronically plagued consumers.

President Ali promises to 'step on the accelerator' in 2023

President of Guyana, Dr Irfaan Ali has promised the nation that his government will 'step on the accelerator' this year, to deliver to and demonstrate to all Guyanese that the riches of the oil and gas industry are manifestly for each and every Guyanese. He clearly understands the impatience that many people feel: they want to see more tangible benefits at the personal and household levels now, rather than later. The talk, the hype, and the euphoria about Guyana's world-leading growth rate in gross domestic product since the advent of oil production have all raised expectations of direct personal benefits for all sections of the population. This has been slow in coming except for those few thousands directly employed by the operators and their sub-contractors and some local businesses. The difference now is that his government has the money to make bold changes at its own speed.

Using the national budget of 2022 as a rough guide, one might get an inkling of the government's fiscal priorities. The 2023 budget should elaborate on this for those interested in the minutiae of government spending. I believe that for healthy public relations a simple table and timeline, showing the full deck of significant new improvements lined up for implementation, and which are directly attributable to the oil revenues, should help to both assure the public that benefits are coming while tempering expectations about how much can be done immediately.

My manifesto: Live, Build, Save, and Give

In July 2019, although a born but now non-Guyanese, I proffered my ideas on a possible allocation and use of the oil revenues at a public talk titled 'Get ready Guyana. You are an Oilman now'. I suggested that the money be divided into four roughly equal baskets called: Live; Build; Save; and Give. The Live basket might be used for immediate improvements in societal necessities such as personal safety, security, health, education, etc. The Build basket might be used for longer-term improvements in infrastructure such as technical colleges, hospitals, roads, bridges, relocation of most of the population to higher ground, a freeport, stadiums, regional parks, a wide rail and truck transportation corridor from the border with Brazil to the Atlantic coast, empolderment of fertile coastal lands for large-scale food production, large power generation plants to facilitate manufacturing, etc. The Save basket was for the sovereign wealth fund, the NRF, to save and invest about a quarter of the oil revenues for when the oil runs out or becomes obsolete and for the benefit of future generations. The fourth basket, Give, is for cash payments to every Guyanese living in Guyana so that everyone benefits directly from the oil and gas industry, lifts many people out of poverty, and help offset some of the inflationary consequences that such a rapid increase in national wealth invariably brings. (The fourth edition of Oil Dorado (2022) goes into more detail on Live, Build, Save and Give.)

The oil and gas revenue stream to Guyana started small in 2020 but will be huge by the tenth year and will continue to be huge for about the following fifteen years as production volumes increase and, more significantly, as the operators' capital costs are paid off by cost recovery from the gross revenues. This will leave more money in the pot for profit-sharing; and will then tail off as the fields become depleted. Of course, in the initial years, most of the oil revenues should be placed in and used for the Live and Build baskets to bring immediate and early improvements in societal conditions and basic national infrastructure.

The time window for Guyana is a little wider and longer

I believe that Guyana's premium oil, cheap to extract and close to major markets, will be in great demand even when fossil fuel becomes second to renewable sources of energy, as will happen over the next two decades. Commercial production of power from hydrogen fusion seems to be about two decades away too. The time window for the beneficial use of oil and gas is shortening because fossil fuels are inherently pollutive, both to extract and consume, and environmentally friendlier alternatives such as wind and solar will provide stiff competition in the future. The time window for Guyana's oil is a little wider and a little longer.

Signature and high-impact projects

The government has initiated several high-visibility, high-impact projects which when completed should transform the lives of all Guyanese. Wider multi-lane highways are being built or are in advanced stages of planning. The rapid increase in the number of automobiles in Guyana in the last decade has shown up the deficiencies of a road system designed more than a century ago. Wider roads entail widening the culverts and bridges, which the roadways cross, over the innumerable creeks and canals that flow to the rivers and the Atlantic Ocean.

A new modern bridge will be built across the Demerara River to replace the old, purely utilitarian floating bridge currently in use. A 300-megawatt electricity plant will be built at the receiving end of a 120-mile-long pipeline transporting associated gas from the Stabroek block to Wales on the West Bank of the Demerara River. Considering that the total national generation of electricity is currently less than 200 megawatts, the increase is huge. The pipeline is big enough to more than double the volume of gas it can transport to the turbines for future expansion.

On another front, to gradually shift power production to eco-friendly sources, plans for a hydroelectric power plant at Amalia Falls have been resuscitated. The plan is to generate 165 megawatts of electricity from this site. Small solar and wind farm projects have been identified but opportunities abound to exploit these readily available sources of renewable power on a massive scale. They are capital-intensive up front but, as the oil revenues mount, the wherewithal to execute these massive projects will be less foreboding.

Two big developments have been announced for Berbice. A new international airport is planned for the Canje-Corentyne districts. A 30,000 barrel per day oil refinery is planned for location on Crab Island which is now nearly completely joined to the mainland of East Berbice by a jubilant growth of mangrove forest. No pipeline has been announced so presumably the crude oil will be brought by tankers from the Stabroek FPSO to the refinery. The products of this refinery are intended for domestic use.

Monetising the rain forest through carbon credits

Guyana is blanketed by one of the largest standing rainforests in the world. Keeping it intact and protecting it from destruction and obliteration makes a significant contribution to the global lung. The logic is that these forests capture carbon dioxide from the air and convert it to oxygen. In effect they are huge chemical plants that do exactly what the world needs: removing excess carbon dioxide from the atmosphere. The bonus is that they do it naturally and do not require massive initial capital outlay. There is inherent value in these carbon credits, which are translatable into cash. An independent agency has verified that Guyana earned 33m tons of carbon credits for the five years 2016 to 2020. Entities wishing to offset their carbon footprint were encouraged to purchase these offsets. The benefit to Guyana is that any sales this year is money immediately earned.

So far, Hess Corp has committed to buy US$750m worth of credits over the next eleven years. They might be considered 'insiders' in the transaction. The true value of Guyana's carbon credits awaits widespread acceptance of the concept by large corporations willing to pay for them. It is conceivable that this might be perceived as a gimmicky ploy or a passing fad, as has befallen some previous attempts at selling carbon credits. Time will tell.

The world price of oil and its impact on Guyana

The amount of money that Guyana gets from oil, both as royalty and profit oil, is entirely dependent on the price of oil and the volume of production. When both the price and the volume are high, royalty is high and profits are higher. This also allows for speedier cost recovery by the operators and it moves forward the date when higher profits are left to be shared between Guyana and the operators. Low price and or low volume do the opposite. It is more beneficial for Guyana to encourage high production rates when the price of oil is high, such as now.

Increasing numbers of Guyanese benefiting directly

Exxon Exploration and Production Guyana Limited (EEPGL), the ExxonMobil subsidiary operating in Guyana on behalf of itself and Hess Corporation and China National Overseas Oil Corporation, recently announced that more than 4,400 Guyanese people were working in support of their operations in Guyana. This is a steady increase over the years. The ripple or trickle-down effects should multiply across the economy and should increase exponentially with increasing exploration and production activities. The expansion in the government's infrastructural projects will add thousands more to the roster of direct beneficiaries as training and education catch up with the demands of bustling industrial and hopefully, agricultural growth. Opportunities abound.

About the contributor

Dr. Tulsi Dyal Singh is a Guyanese-born American. He has lived in Midland, Texas since 1979. He is a former president of the board of trustees of the Permian Basin Petroleum Museum, Library and Hall of Fame. He was honoured as Outstanding Philanthropist of the Year in 2001 and as Person of Vision in 2002. Dr. Singh has degrees in Medicine and Health Care Administration and is a certified bank director through the Southwestern Graduate School of Banking.

Chapter Four

All that glisters is not black gold: The CGX story

John Mair tells the sad tale of a first mover that may become a first outer

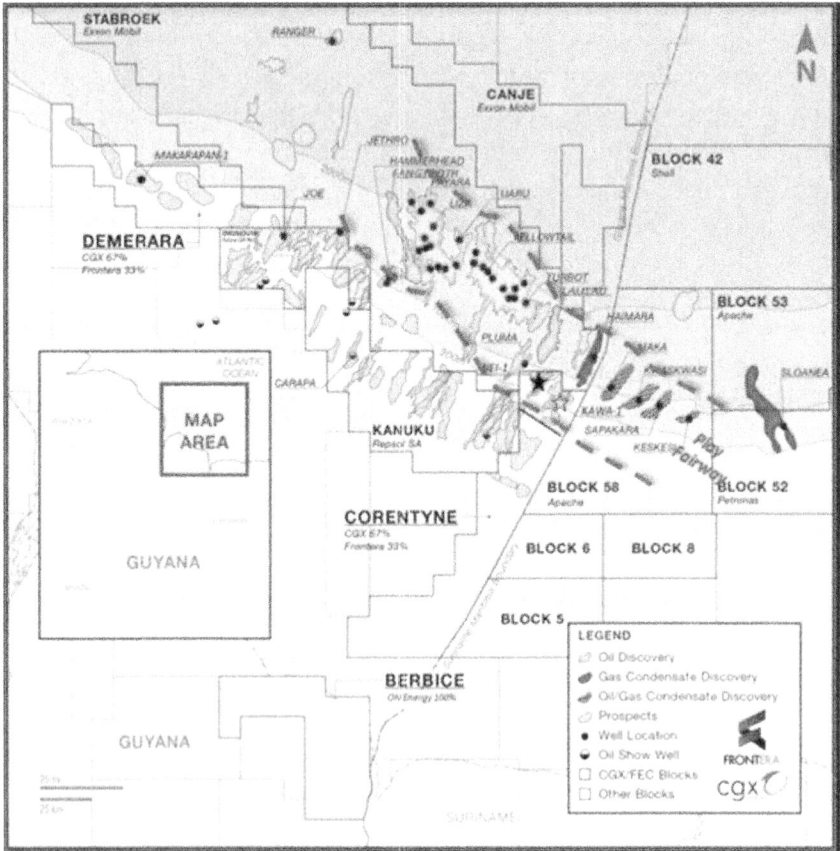

Source: CGX

CGX should be one of the major success stories of the Guyana oil boom. They are not, and like the Black Knight in Monty Python and the Holy Grail who has every limb hacked off bit by bit, they are having to sell off limb after limb to others to stay in the oil exploration business. It seems a sad story. How did they get there?

Let's go back to Guyana oil pre-history. 1998. The company was formed in Canada by John Cullen and Guyanese emigré Idres K Dookie. CGX were the first movers in Guyana oil. In June 2000 they set up an exploratory rig in the disputed area between Guyana and Suriname. They were chased off by the Surinamese navy. That caused great regional tension. I was working for then President Jagdeo at the time and experienced it first-hand. The chickens were losing their heads.

Guyana had (and still has) no navy to speak of so, instead, they took the Surinam Bouterse government to an international court, citing the Laws of the Seas Convention. They engaged high-level and expensive lawyers, led by former Commonwealth Secretary General and Guyanese Sir Shridath 'Sonny' Ramphal. That litigation is said to have cost US$5m, with finance allegedly provided by CGX. The Guyana government won the case in 2007. Under the final judgement, Guyana was given 93 per cent of the area under dispute and they could start thinking of exploiting that section of their offshore oil resources.

Jagdeo grateful?

Then President Jagdeo, today the Guyana oil supremo, and his government were deeply indebted to them. They were given three areas to explore with the New Demerara Petroleum Agreement, the New Berbice Petroleum Agreement and the Corentyne Petroleum Agreement in 2012/2013 (see map above).

CGX continued to try to find commercial oil offshore and onshore, but they were still late to the party and oil finding is an expensive business. Two wells were drilled on their Corentyne block licence Another well, Jaguar-1, was drilled in February 2012 on the Georgetown block but was subsequently abandoned due to safety concerns. Eagle-1 was drilled months later, but the results there too were disappointing.

All costs and no revenue so far for CGX.

What CGX had:

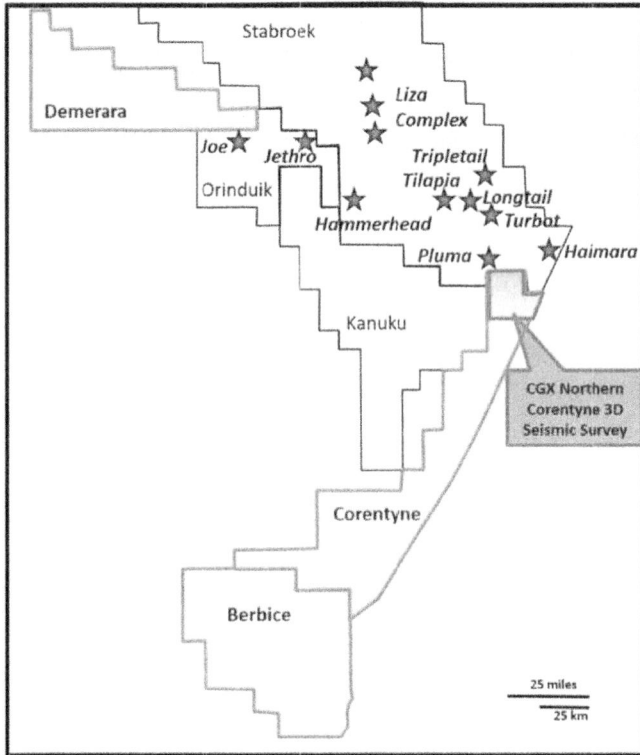

Source: CGX

Turbulence above the surface

CGX itself meanwhile was going through ructions. Founder Idris K Dookie, by now an almost permanent feature at Pegasus Hotel poolside in Georgetown entertaining clients (this author noted he had two mobile phones which he certainly regarded as 'interesting'), was deposed in a palace coup in March 2013. In 2022, he is still bitter at what he told me were 'the traitors'.

CGX itself soldiered on whilst admitting they were in dire financial straits. One company, Pacific Rubales Energy, was being offered 70 per cent of CGX in return for a capital infusion of $15m. That deal did not materialise.

Boom but bust for CGX

The Guyana oil boom proper did not start until May 2015 when ExxonMobil struck oil big in the Stabroek field. CGX had licences in the adjacent fields. Those were proving fallow but, despite that, CGX continued exploring and spending money in pursuit of the oil Holy Grail. By now the company had a new chair/CEO in Professor Suresh Narine, a young tyro Canadian/Guyanese academic.

But still no oil

Turbulence and new brooms in the boardroom did not bring any better results offshore.

Light at the end of the tunnel: Jagdeo still grateful?

In February 2022, just in time for the biggest oil/gas conference ever held in Guyana, CGX finally struck oil at the Kawi well in their Corentyne block. It came with a cost. To fund the further exploration of the Wei-1 well and Kawi wells they had to relinquish shares in the company to Frontera Energy.

In return for $160m of injected capital CGX gave up two-thirds of the company. Some of that amount was repayment for monies borrowed on convertible loans from Frontera in 2021 and 2022. The deal meant that Frontera became the operator of the Corentyne licence with a 68 per cent stake, while CGX retained the remaining 32 per cent working interest.

More limbs sacrificed

It was said that Bharrat Jagdeo, now the oil supremo, was losing patience with his erstwhile friends.

In June 2022 he announced that, given their inability to honour their work obligations, Frontera Energy Corporation and CGX Energy Inc. had reached an agreement with the Guyana government to relinquish the Demerara and Berbice Blocks, amounting to a combined 1.1 million acres. Two-thirds gone.

More limbs amputated. But oil was on its way. Was it?

Drilling of Wei-1 exploration well was set to take place in October 2022. That deadline kept slipping towards 2023.

Twenty-two years on: Diversification?

CGX today is operator of just the Corentyne block. Partners Frontera Energy Corporation hold a two-thirds interest while CGX hold just a third interest. It was still not all plain sailing to profit from oil though. CGX announced that the opening-up of the Wei-1 well had shifted from quarter three to quarter four in 2022. It is thought for financial/cost flow reasons.

Twenty years and no commercial oil to date. Losses were mounting. CGX Energy Inc. announced on 10 August that for the first half of the year 2022 it has recorded almost US$7m in losses. compared with a net loss of US $3.4m for the same period in 2021. CGX were quite simply running out of limbs to sacrifice.
One last delay?

Suresh Narine had also proudly announced at that February 2022 conference the building by CGX of a deep-water port in Berbice. He showed the audience detailed plans for it. The deep- water port facility is intended to serve as an offshore supply base for the oil and gas industry and as a multi-purpose terminal cargo handling base to service agricultural import/export, containerised, and specialized cargo. The BDWP aims to enable provisioning of operators and vendors in territorial waters of both Guyana and Suriname.

But today even that sideshow looks like going sour as Guyana President Ali told the company in August 2022 to get a move on with that project or lose it. He had other investors waiting on the sidelines ready and willing to build the facility and to profit from it. CGX announced in the same month that the building of that deep-water port was behind schedule. To date, they have spent US$22m on the BDWP. It has yet to open.

Not quite the end

On 1 December 2022, in another new announcement about the Frontera/CGX's Black Gold (Black Hole?) offshore CGX said it was postponing drilling of the Wei-1 well in offshore Guyana, citing contractor obligations elsewhere. They said they had agreed with the Guyanese government to start drilling no later than 31 January 2023 to allow contractor Noble Corp Plc to complete current obligations in Trinidad.

The future onshore is not bright. Offshore there is a little more hope. From oil heroes to oil near zeroes in two decades. Few limbs are left to amputate. The body now belongs to others. It may be just a corpse. That sadly, is the CGX story.

Chapter Five

'Oil Dorado' in 'One Guyana'

Geoffrey Da Silva is an insider turned outsider. He was a minister in a previous PPP/C government, then Ambassador to Venezuela from 2011 to 2015. Now he lives in Canada and takes a more dispassionate view of the oil bonanza

Many Guyanese citizens are yet to be convinced that, over the next 25 years, we will achieve national unity and successfully avoid or overcome the negative financial, economic, social, and political effects of the nation's major challenges and threats such as:

- the resource curse ('Dutch Disease');

- climate change with degradation of the coastal and marine environments, massive floods and droughts;

- the political stalemate: in the 2011, 2015, and 2020 national elections, the two major political parties (PPP/C and APNU/AFC) won the tiniest possible majorities in Parliament (by only one seat and by an advantage of less than 2 per cent of total votes);

- inter-ethnic suspicions that sometimes lead to physical violence, especially against Indo-Guyanese;

- a very high poverty rate (43.4 per cent of the population – 338,520 persons) among the seven ethnic communities of Indigenous (Amerindian), African, Indian, Mixed, Portuguese, Chinese, and European ancestry; and

- significant corruption in the public and private sectors.

How to meet those challenges

With regards to the first major challenge, Guyana does not (presently) have the resource curse. President Irfaan Ali's government has begun to implement pro-poor and pro-business economic, financial, social, and political policies to avoid the 'Dutch

Disease' and meet the 'basic needs of every single Guyanese', so that no individual or family is left behind.

Many infrastructure projects are presently underway in many communities. In each of the country's ten regions, there are new housing areas with infrastructure and utilities, especially for low and middle-income-earners. Emphasis is being placed on developing a resilient, competitive, and diversified private sector economy, including micro, small, and medium-sized businesses. In the hinterland communities, most Indigenous (Amerindian) Guyanese communities are experiencing economic, social, and cultural development. Across the country, there is modernization of the education, health, sports, and recreational sectors.

The root causes of the 'resource curse'

But avoiding the 'Dutch Disease' will be easier said than done. Like the PPP/C government, governments in most oil-producing countries had similar good intentions, yet many of these countries became more underdeveloped and poorer because most of their political and private sector leaders denied, ignored, downplayed, or misunderstood the symptoms that could indicate whether the root causes of the 'resource curse' existed in their countries.

Public investments and public spending

A root cause of the 'Dutch Disease' is when a government does not efficiently and effectively manage its public investments and public spending system (PIMS).

There are already symptoms that this could happen in Guyana. According to the International Monetary Fund, Guyana's PIMS is 1.5 times less efficient than those in most countries of Latin America and the Caribbean. With the increasing inflow of massive funds from the oil sector, the government will have to patiently expand its PIMS to avoid overheating the economy, to keep inflation at low levels, and to ensure that the foreign exchange rate does not reach a level that would negatively affect the export opportunities for products and services from the non-oil economic sectors. The focus must be on continuously monitoring, evaluating, and adjusting the capacities of both the public sector and the private sector to absorb public investments and public spending. As those absorption capacities grow every year, the inflow of funds into those sectors could be increased. If this is not done, Guyana will experience 'debt distress' similar to what another new oil-producing country, Ghana, is presently experiencing. (See chapter twenty-six of this book.)

Fundamentally, the government has to publicly and transparently outline its financing plan so that every single Guyanese will know:

- how economic and social programmes will be expanded and sustained over the next 25 years;

- how development funds will be sourced at the lowest possible interest rates,

- how the increasing public debt will be managed;

- how the oversight of major projects will be improved to avoid missed deadlines and significant cost overruns;

- how the tax base will be diversified to prevent over-dependence on oil revenues,

- how both foreign and local investors will be encouraged to reinvest most of their profits into the national economy; and

- how the anti-corruption programme will be effectively implemented in all government institutions.

A new export strategy for non-oil sectors

Another root cause of the 'Dutch Disease' is when most of the local and foreign private investments are happening in activities connected to the oil and gas sector. There are already symptoms that this could happen in Guyana. Most of the new large local and foreign investments are in oil-related businesses supported by the government's aggressive local content policies. At the same time, there are increases of all kinds of imports, including raw materials and foods that could be produced in the country.

In the beginning, this is expected and understandable because Guyana is a very new oil producer. However, if that initial imbalance continues for many years in favour of oil-related over non-oil investments, the export of crude oil will become an overwhelming share of all exports, as has happened in most underdeveloped oil-producing countries where there is little economic diversification.

Presently, there is considerable positive growth in construction, housing, and other non-oil economic activities. However, Guyana has a relatively small local market. Balanced growth of the oil and the non-oil sectors will depend on a significant increase of exports by micro, small, medium, and large businesses from the non-oil sectors. In addition to its local content policies, the government, in partnership with the private sector, has to begin the design of a new export strategy that prioritises the establishment or enhancement of effective export promotion institutions that will support non-oil businesses to expand in current export markets and enter into new export markets with value-added products and services. A data-driven and integrated export strategy is one of the key 'secrets' that successful oil-producing countries use to diversify their economies.

Poverty reduction, job creation, and immigration

Other root causes of 'Dutch Disease' are failure to reduce poverty and high unemployment, especially among youth and women, and failure to implement a well-managed and targeted immigration policy. There are already symptoms that this could happen in Guyana. We are yet to see a comprehensive programme to measure and reduce deep poverty across and within the ethnic communities. A significant wage gap exists between females and males who perform the same work of equal value, and there is a wide income gap between executives and employees in the public and private sectors.

At least 344,000 Guyanese (out of 780,000 people who live in the country) are below or near the poverty line. These citizens cannot afford, like the upper middle class and the rich, to buy private healthcare and private education, and they do not own cars, electric generators (to deal with the many power outages), or water-purifying systems.

With regard to job creation, the government must be commended for its innovative programme to help families cope with the rising cost of living by hiring 11,000 people to do part-time jobs in the public sector. But massively expanding the number of people employed in the public sector by at least 21 per cent is not sustainable, and this programme could become an unintended waste of precious human and financial resources.

Only a government/business/trade union partnership could find the best solutions to overcome the existing labour shortages in some non-oil sectors and the high unemployment in specific regions and communities. The focus of that partnership should be to promote fair competition for labour between businesses in the non-oil sectors, the oil and gas sector, and the public sector. That public/private partnership also has to urgently design and implement a new immigration plan to reverse the continuing 'brain drain' by promoting 'brain circulation' from the diaspora and by selectively managing the recruitment of skilled foreign employees.

Expanding public consultation, transforming public sector institutions, and improving data collection and analysis.

Other root causes of the 'Dutch Disease' are:

- failure to build a national consensus through regular public consultations and dialogue on a country's top investment priorities and on the sequencing of major transformational projects,

- failure to implement a programme, in partnership with communities and non-governmental organisations (trade unions, business organisations, community groups, religious bodies and charities) that promotes an anti-corruption culture in government institutions to make them more accessible, inclusive, transparent, accountable, incorruptible, efficient, and effective by using new thinking, staff incentives, and new training, and

- failure to improve data collection and analysis so that policy-makers at the national, regional and community levels could make more informed decisions.

Changing the Petroleum Production Sharing Agreements (PSAs)

A major root cause of the 'Dutch Disease' is the failure to change a PSA where and when it is necessary. A government/non-governmental partnership has to be forged to change those onerous and unfair terms in the 2016 PSA that was signed between the then APNU/AFC Government of Guyana and ExxonMobil and its partners (Hess Corporation of the USA and CNOOC Petroleum Limited of China).

It is normal practice in the petroleum industry for either a government or an oil company to request changes in a PSA. In the interest of fairness for both parties in the 2016 PSA, the government and Exxon (with its partners), have to compromise and change the sections that deal with the non-payment of corporate income taxes, the low royalty rate, the lack of ring-fencing, the short timelines for auditing production costs, and the insufficient insurance coverage to protect the marine and land environments.

The most urgent priority for the government is to establish a Petroleum Commission to ensure effective oversight of the oil and gas industry.

A people's 'Oil Dorado'?

'Oil Dorado' must not be a financial bonanza just for American, Canadian, Chinese, European, and Trinidadian oil companies, and a small multi-ethnic elite made up of some Guyanese businesspeople, politicians, and officials.

The overwhelming majority of Guyanese want a people's 'Oil Dorado' where there are equal opportunities so that not one individual or family is left behind. The priority must be to ensure that all workers, farmers, the unemployed, the marginalized, the poor, and the hungry will enjoy higher income levels, improved social services, and better living standards.

For this to happen:

- all members and supporters of the governing PPP/C political party, not just its leaders, must take primary responsibility for genuinely and humbly reaching out to all grassroots communities to overcome the political stalemate and the ethnic fears and stereotypes, and

- Guyanese in all ethnic communities, regardless of ethnicity, gender, age, religion, class, disability or political affiliation, must actively become involved in the design and implementation of the 'One Guyana' policies of President Ali's government.

Note on contributor

Geoffrey Da Silva is a former Government of Guyana Minister and was the Ambassador to Venezuela from 2011 to 2015.

Chapter Six

The Venezuela border controversy: Diplomacy must continue to complement the ICJ process

Former Ambassador Riyad Insanally calls for enhanced diplomacy to complement Guyana's case before the International Court of Justice, aimed at resolving the border controversy with Venezuela. Between 17 and 22 November 2022 the International Court of Justice (ICJ) heard submissions from Guyana and Venezuela on the latter's objections to Guyana's case seeking to uphold the validity and binding nature of the 1899 Arbitral Award which established the land border between the two countries

The Guyana Government viewed Venezuela's preliminary objections to the admissibility of the case, which resulted in a suspension of the substantive hearing of the case, as a deliberate delaying tactic. Guyana's international legal team nonetheless presented Guyana's position on Venezuela's objections most competently and with consummate professionalism.

No room for complacency

Guyana, quite correctly, places its faith in the rule of international law. While there is cautious optimism that the outstanding team of international lawyers can deliver a favourable result for Guyana, there can be no room for complacency, especially in the face of increased Venezuelan diplomatic activity, along with an escalated social media campaign, all aimed at presenting – or misrepresenting – Venezuela as the wronged party in the 1899 settlement of the border.

Guyana cannot rely only the strength of legal arguments. Diplomacy must continue to complement the ICJ process. President Irfaan Ali said as much in his Independence Day address in May 2022, stating that Guyana would not 'deviate from the judicial path' while continuing 'to marshal the best diplomatic efforts necessary to ensure respect for all our territorial space'.

This is arguably the most critical existential issue faced by Guyana since independence in 1966. Lacking in economic clout or military might, the young nation deployed some of its finest minds in pursuing diplomacy as its first line of defence against the Venezuelan threat to its sovereignty and territorial integrity. Now, almost six decades later and with the country poised for a massive economic transformation, there can be no lessening of the diplomatic effort, even as the lawyers fight the case at the ICJ.

The diplomatic imperative

Guyana cannot afford to underestimate the threat posed by a Venezuela divided by bitter politics and riven by all sorts of economic and social problems. The episodic sabre-rattling next door may be meant to distract Venezuelans from their daily woes but the one thing that unites the opposing parties in Venezuela is the mistaken belief that Essequibo is 'theirs'. The massive oil reserves being discovered offshore Guyana have only served to intensify their lust for Guyana's territory and maritime area.

Thus, both the Maduro regime and the opposition have sought to outdo each other in nationalistic, anti-Guyana rhetoric, actively promoting their self-serving and fallacious interpretations of the 1899 Award, the Geneva Agreement, and the ICJ process.

Successive Guyana Governments have been ever cognisant of Venezuelan propaganda and its reach. Now, more than ever, the Venezuelan narrative must be countered with nimble and proactive diplomacy, to keep allies onside, to keep informed those who would prefer to sit on the fence, and to neutralise those who are not so favourably disposed towards Guyana. This is the diplomatic imperative.

It should therefore be standard operating procedure for the political leadership, diplomatic representatives, and other government officials to present, at every opportunity – in multilateral forums, bilateral meetings, academic settings, think tanks and so on – the truth about the 1899 Award, even as they remain alert to Venezuela's propensity for spreading misinformation.

In the latter respect, it is commendable that Foreign Secretary Robert Persaud wrote to Facebook and Twitter, in October 2022, requesting that they remove posts with illegal maps claiming Guyana's territory. Indeed, this awareness of what is propagated in cyberspace needs to be taken to another level. If not already contemplated, a unit with Spanish language skills should be established at the Foreign Ministry to monitor and counter Venezuelan fake news.

The Chilean experience

Nothing can be taken for granted, either at the national or international level. Unity of purpose and message is absolutely essential. The experience of Chile in the maritime dispute with Peru, settled by the ICJ in 2014, is instructive. Here are a few of the lessons learned from informal engagements with key members of Chile's legal team.

While the issue is predominantly a legal one, it is also very much a political one. Chile created a bipartisan team of lawyers and historians to shape the national narrative. There were meetings of former presidents and foreign ministers aimed at informing strategy and reinforcing the national consensus. There were also periodic briefings and a process of consultation at the national level, which involved all sectors, particularly the Supreme Court, the armed forces, academia, and civil society. All this took place because national unity was deemed to be of the utmost strategic importance in the presentation of Chile's position to the international community. In Guyana's case, national unity on the border controversy is not in doubt and should be reinforced whenever and wherever possible.

Reinforcing the narrative and enhanced diplomacy

While the integrity of the ICJ judges is not in question, it has to be recognised that election to the Court is still a political process. In this context, knowledge about the composition of the Court and the nationalities of the judges is very important. Guyana should seek to develop closer relations with the countries from which the judges come. One is not suggesting that the judges would be easily swayed by political considerations but reinforcing one's case with the power of diplomacy and presenting Guyana in the most positive light should not be underestimated.

With political considerations always a factor, Guyana's narrative has to be continuously and forcefully repeated at every possible opportunity, as an overriding foreign policy imperative.
Guyana should advance its position and cause in all multilateral groupings to which it belongs, such as the Caribbean Community, the Commonwealth, the Non-Aligned Movement, and the Organisation of African, Caribbean and Pacific States. For it should always be borne in mind that Venezuela's reach in the developing world is still long.

Regarding the Latin American neighbourhood, Guyana has to tread carefully. Ever since joining the Organization of American States (OAS) in 1991, successive governments have deliberately kept the border controversy away from the ambit of that organisation, wary of Latin solidarity with Venezuela. Guyana's diplomats should be ever vigilant, not only with regard to the OAS but also with the Community of Latin American and Caribbean States, the Association of Caribbean States and, quite possibly, a revived Union of South American Nations, even as Guyana's new status as a quickly growing oil producer and an emerging player in ensuring Latin American and Caribbean energy security could help to change the equation in Guyana's favour.

When UN Secretary General Ban Ki-Moon was considering whether or not to pass the controversy to the ICJ for settlement and when his successor, Antônio Guterres, made the decision to do so, a significant factor was the quiet backing of key powers in helping the UN authorities arrive at a decision based not only on international law and a strict interpretation of the UN Charter and the Geneva Agreement but also one which would enjoy widespread political acceptance. Now that the case is before the ICJ, there should be no diminishing of diplomatic efforts to reinforce the merits of Guyana's case. For, if the Court rules in Guyana's favour, the weight of international opinion will have to be relied upon to get Venezuela to accept the judgement.

While the government is investing resources in building capacity to manage the new oil and gas sector effectively, a relatively small portion of the oil windfall could be spent on training a new cadre of diplomats to beef up Guyana's efforts to counter the Venezuelan threat. Enhanced diplomacy should be the order of the day; indeed, it will continue to be necessary well into the future.

This is a version of an article that first appeared on the OilNOW website on 13 November 2022.

About the contributor

Dr Riyad Insanally CCH was a career diplomat for 31 years and last served as Guyana's Ambassador to the United States of America and Permanent Representative to the Organization of American States from September 2016 to June 2021. He is currently a Senior Fellow at the Caribbean Initiative of the Atlantic Council's Adrienne Arsht Latin America Center in Washington, DC. He holds MA and MPhil degrees from the University of Cambridge, and a PhD from Harvard University.

Chapter Seven

Why is China interested in Guyana's oil?

The China National Offshore Oil Corporation (CNOOC) is a big player in the offshore Guyana oil boom. CNOOC Petroleum Guyana holds 25 per cent of the prolific Stabroek Block. Is this initiative Belt and Road, belt and braces, or just a sensible early investment? Jungi Yan and Ali Hasan Humza, of the Communication University of China, discuss the issues raised by China's developing relationship with Guyana

China has been investing heavily in developing economies globally. The foundation of any strong economic relationship hinges on mutual collaboration, trustworthiness, and time-tested reliability on both sides. In what follows we will offer an in-depth investigation into the historical significance of Guyana's oil industry and China's reasons for fostering a strong economic relationship with Guyana, specifically in oil exploration and production.

The world picture

In the past decade, more than 4,360 oil and gas discoveries have been made worldwide, including 234.9bn barrels of oil equivalent. Among them, 37 major oil and gas discoveries with more than 1bn barrels of oil equivalent (about 140 million tons) have been made, and new discoveries have reached 86.3bn barrels of oil equivalent. This accounts for 37 per cent of all new global oil and gas discoveries. The 37 discoveries, mostly on both sides of the Atlantic Ocean and in the Persian Gulf, accounted for 90 per cent of the world's major new discoveries. Large discoveries on both sides of the Atlantic and the Persian Gulf accounted for 76 per cent of global reserves between 2010 and 2020. Seven discoveries were made on both sides of the Atlantic Ocean, while Brazil, Guyana, and the United States accounted for nearly half of the total with 16. The two biggest discoveries are the Liza field in Guyana, and the Faihaa field in Iraq.

Stabroek pays off

The Liza oil and gas field in Guyana and the Stabroek block are the focus of investments in South America by multinational companies such as ExxonMobil. The extraordinary discoveries in Guyana and neighbouring South America will rewrite the future of these developing countries.

As early as 1991, western consortiums led by ExxonMobil entered Guyana for oil exploration, but early failures made some investors withdraw. ExxonMobil persisted because the government of Guyana offered favourable risk terms.

In May 2015, ExxonMobil discovered oil more than 6,500 metres deep and 150 metres thick in the Canya Formation mudstone cretaceous sandstone in the Deepwater Liza field. It holds as much oil as the entire Gulf of Mexico. The discovery opened the door to riches and, since then other huge discoveries have been made in Guyana and the adjacent waters of Suriname.

ExxonMobil, Hess, and CNOOC hold, respectively, 45 per cent, 30 per cent, and 25 per cent interests in the Stabroek block. In 2012 CNOOC acquired Canada's Nexen, which in 2007 had acquired the interest for participating in ExxonMobil's venture exploration project in Guyana.

After ExxonMobil announced its discovery in 2015 and brought up first oil in 2019, the country rapidly became an oil upstart. Benefiting from the oil boom, the economy begun to experience unprecedented growth. After achieving 43 per cent growth in 2020 and 20 per cent growth in 2021, the GDP of the country is set to have grown by a remarkable 49 per cent in 2022 as their oil reserves and production soar. With a population of only about 800,000, Guyana is likely to overtake Kuwait as the world's largest per-capita oil producer by 2025.

CNOOC is part of Guyana's oil boom

By May 2022, a consortium of ExxonMobil, Hess, and CNOOC had discovered more than thirty large oil and gas fields off the coast of Guyana with estimated recoverable reserves of 11bn barrels today, up from 1.5bn barrels when oil was first discovered in 2015. The IMF forecasts that the country's output will rise from 340,000 b/d (barrels per day) in 2022 to 1m b/d or more in 2027, raising it to eleventh in world rankings of countries producing more than 1m b/d.

The country's oil is high-quality, sweet, light crude oil, which is cheap to produce and can be sold at break-even prices as low as US$25 a barrel, making it extremely cost-effective. This compares favourably with world oil prices.

In December 2022, Guyana's President Ali announced a tender for offshore blocks that could provide another twenty-five billion barrels of potential crude oil reserves. It is the country's first competitive offshore block tender. The country's discoveries have been labelled the fastest-growing 'Superbasin', attracting the attention of global oil investors.

China and Guyana: a long history

Guyana is rich in natural resources but small in population. During British colonial rule, the construction of transportation, energy, and other infrastructure was stagnant, and its economic and social development lagged considerably. The country became independent in 1966, and in 1970 Guyana's parliament decided to abolish the Queen as head of state and declared itself a republic.

In June 1972, the governments of China and Guyana formally announced the establishment of diplomatic relations. Guyana was the first country in the Caribbean to establish relations with China as well as being the first among Latin American countries to do. Chinese people have made important contributions to the development of Guyana. This has been recognised by the Guyana government who announced in 2017 that 12 January would be in future designated as the Chinese Arrival Day in Guyana.

Despite the Covid pandemic, Guyana's gross domestic product expanded by 43.5 per cent in 2020, and, according to the International Monetary Fund, grew by 20 per cent in 2021 when oil reserves and production surged. Guyana's rapid economic growth is gaining momentum. The IMF expects the country's GDP to grow by a remarkable 49 per cent in 2022 as oil reserves and production soar. Guyana is expected to pump more than 1m barrels of crude oil a day by 2028, becoming the eleventh country in the world to reach that figure.

The success of the Guyana oil project would not only revolutionise the country's economic model, but it would also set it on a path to prosperity. Since China's reform and opening up in the 1980s, the focus of China's energy demand has been to rapidly increase the scale of energy production and consumption based on the needs of rapid economic development and to establish a relatively stable energy supply system.

China has had a sizeable advantage of infrastructure capacity and the energy demand that leads to the development of advanced developed countries, and Guyana has the energy advantage but a backward level of infrastructure construction. It may be surmised that both sides can complement each other's advantages and disadvantages. Guyana will become a rising energy star in South America, and China will obtain another stable energy supply channel.

The future

China has a great demand for energy, minerals, and strong infrastructure capacity, which are complementary to the economic development of Guyana. Benefiting from China's One Belt, One Road strategy, Chinese-funded enterprises have made contributions to the country's economic and social development. Large local infrastructure facilities, such as the Cheddi Jagan airport expansion, the east coast Demerara highway reconstruction, and national broadband, have been built by Chinese-funded enterprises, creating a large number of job opportunities for Guyanese. Bosai Mining has developed into the second-largest bauxite mining company in Guyana, becoming the main economic pillar and tax source for Linden. Given the huge potential of oil and gas exploration and development in the country, CNOOC's harvest, and the good exchanges and cooperation between the two countries in the past, the sector is expected to attract more Chinese investment in the near future.

China has also been active in other areas of the economy in Guyana such as agriculture and tourism. Chinese companies have invested in agricultural projects helping to improve agricultural productivity and efficiency. The strong ties between China and Guyana have resulted in a marked increase in tourism in recent years as well. Chinese tourists travel to Guyana and contribute to its tourism industry.

Finally, the two countries have also strengthened their political and diplomatic ties. This also helps with economic aspects as both countries have worked together in multilateral forums such as the United Nations and the Caribbean Community.
Overall, in our view, the economic relationship between China and Guyana has been mutually beneficial and has helped to improve the economic well-being of both countries. It looks promising for the future as well as both countries are keen to further expand the relationship and aim to be dependable strategic partners in the oil and energy sector.

About the contributors

Junqi Yan is a professor in CUC's School of Economics and Management. He previously worked for PetroChina as a systems analyst.

Ali Hasan Humza works as general manager for Beijing Yixin Qinxi Psychology Ltd. He used to work for Well Manufacturing Services China (Shell & CNPC J.V) as operations manager.

Chapter Eight
Getting from here to there: Guyana's Oil Dorado journey

Professor Anthony T. Bryan, a longtime observer of Guyanese oil and gas, looks at how boom came to Guyana and the dangers it brought

In January 2023 the constant media cacophony about Guyana's emergence as an oil and gas economy is boisterous and overwhelming. Here are some examples: 'Guyana and Suriname have reached developmental "take-off" speed' (OilNOW, 31 May 2021); 'Guyana enters the big league as O&G revenues break $1 billion in 2022, grow to $7.5 billion in 2030' (Rystad Energy, 22 July 2022); and 'Booming Guyana only country in the region to record double- digit growth in 2023' (World Bank, 10 January 2023).

Enthusiasm is justified, and the authors document their analysis with statistical evidence. But the hyperbole in the headlines runs the risk of raising public expectations to an uncomfortable level. So perhaps it is time for retrospection, a reality check, and a cautionary note. After all, this is what this new edition of Oil Dorado sets out to do.

In the beginning

I started writing and publishing about Guyana's oil and gas potential as early as 2011 after the discovery of the Zaedyus well offshore French Guiana. The Zaedyus well proved that the Jubilee-play, a huge discovery offshore Ghana in West Africa, was mirrored on the other side of the Atlantic. This 'Atlantic Mirror' discovery opened a new hydrocarbon basin within which the deep sea of neighbouring countries such as Guyana and Suriname could be mapped and reduce the exploration risk associated with prospective inventory offshore. Although there still are no subsequent discoveries offshore French Guiana, the story is different for its neighbours.

We are aware of Guyana's good fortune with respect to oil and gas discoveries. In a widely distributed op-ed (1 March 2021) in the Guyanese publication OilNOW I described the Guyana-Suriname Basin (GSB) as the 'Holy Grail' of oil and gas in the Americas (and in the second edition of Oil Dorado too).

Hyperbole headline yes (mea culpa), but the facts were accurate.

A reality check

Here are prognostications, even at the risk of stating the obvious.

First, Guyana is not slowing down on its energy boom. The government has said so. Guyana's oil reserves are vast. They are estimated at 11bn barrels of recoverable oil -- one of the highest levels per capita worldwide. The country's daily production (b/d) is projected to rise from the December 2022 level of 360,000 b/d to 750,000 b/d by 2025 and, by 2027, more than one million b/d of oil equivalent. At that point Guyana will surpass Kuwait which is presently the nation with the highest level of production per capita on the planet. Some estimates suggest that the size and extent of Guyana's offshore oil fields are larger than those of Norway and Oman.

Although Guyana only produced its first barrels of oil in December 2019, it is on track to boast the globe's highest GDP growth rate of 2022 -- a remarkable 57.8 percent.

Second,_dealing with this windfall is a new experience for the Guyanese government and its people. Until the first discovery, Guyana had no known oil reserves, unlike its immediate neighbours Trinidad and Venezuela (both have been oil producers for more than a century), Suriname and Brazil. Now it is racing to provide the necessary legislation, to create the institutional structures, and to devise strategies to manage an oil economy.

Obviously, the looming pitfall is the dreaded 'resource curse' or the 'paradox of plenty' where destabilization of traditional economic sectors occur as the country becomes overly dependent on exports of a single commodity. That is why Venezuela, Nigeria, and some major emerging oil producers are experiencing failed economies. Some economically poor but resource-rich countries tend to be less developed precisely because of the inflationary consequences of their resource wealth. In some circles, oil is known as the 'excrement of the devil'. Although international credit agencies report that Guyana has a low level of corruption, regulations must be developed to control that elephant in the room which is running loose in some emerging oil states.

The government must ensure that the country has all the contractual provisions in place to earn its fair share of the windfall. The population can become frustrated by the lack of any immediate tangible benefits that they may have expected from oil revenues. Guyana could become one of the world's richest nations per capita but managing public expectations is critical, or a crisis of expectations can have a negative impact on the country's ability to meet its goals. Similarly, the possibility of political and ethnic strife is a constant threat if the benefits of the windfall are not distributed evenly among the various ethnic groups.

Third, the impact of the oil and gas windfall on Guyana's economy can be convulsive. It will grow exponentially. Independent analyst group Rystad Energy estimates that national revenue will amount to more than US$117bn over the lifetime of the projects. Managing the windfall presents many challenges.

An early IDB Quarterly Report (21 December 2020) pointed out that Guyana can plunge itself into more debt even with the surplus oil money. So the IDB is advising the government to save for a rainy day and to exercise caution in the way in which it goes about taking on new loans. Oil revenues will give the government an opportunity to close budget financing gaps, to avoid debt accumulation, and to retire expensive outstanding public debt. Budget financing needs to be monitored; savings must not be eroded; if they are this could return the country to high indebtedness.

In a recent release published by Reuters (27 September 2022) the IMF urges cautious policies even as the nation benefits from surging oil production. The IMF notes that while surging oil output could help address development needs and buffer the economy, it also faces risks from volatile oil prices, a slowing global economy, and possible difficulties managing the resource. The IMF directors have 'highlighted the need for continued prudent policies and structural reforms, assisted by Fund technical assistance'.

Fourth, the key to Guyana's success is the effective management of the oil and gas sector. Oversight, transparency, and timely information for the public about expected income flows and expenditures are best practices for the successful management of the sector. To their credit, Government officials have stated that the essential hallmarks of the policy must be accountability, realistic targets, opportunities for capacity building, and incentives that allow that the Guyanese people to benefit the most from their oil wealth.

The country's political leaders have also emphasized that certain services should be reserved for Guyanese procurement since the bulk of the benefits cannot just go to the investors -- the people of Guyana must be given ample opportunity to share in the prosperity. The local content law seeks to protect local Guyanese companies. While this is a commendable objective, just filling percentage workforce with nationals in the name of 'local content' is a mistake to be avoided. This is not about numbers; it's about investing in the long-term benefits for the country and its people.

Moving forward: investment

As Guyana moves forward to being Oil Dorado, there are positives and negatives. Clearly, attaining high-income status from natural resource wealth does not always translate into improved human development outcomes. There are many 'above-ground' pitfalls but at present there are very positive signs that Guyana is going in the right direction.

With respect to investment, there are opportunities for international capital to make long-term investments along the entire oil and gas value chain. And there are potentially even more indirect opportunities that arise when the country starts to exponentially increase its GDP and raise the income level of the entire nation.

Theoretically, the investment opportunities are as broad as one's imagination or skill set. But part of the transformation demands collaboration with foreign investors and building a Guyanese mindset that is open to foreign investment rather than resisting it out of fear of foreign domination as in colonial times. However, it takes years for changes to trickle down and for processes to be streamlined to overcome Guyana's legacy of tight state control. Progress is being made and ways must be found to keep up the momentum of change.

Globally, investment is slowing down in new oil provinces, but Guyana's light sweet crude is an exception to the trend. Its energy resources are attracting a lot of investment but there are lots of investment opportunities in the non-oil sectors as well. Unfortunately, the focus on oil and gas exploration can divert the attention of foreign investors and multinational enterprises from other promising sectors and industries that could strengthen the Guyanese economy. Upstream activities such as oil services, equipment, transportation, and technology tied to the petroleum sector offer abundant opportunities for companies and entrepreneurs doing business in the energy sector. These provide a multiplier effect that is important to the development of the Guyanese economy and its people.

Since there is agreement among CARICOM leaders that the vast agricultural land mass of Guyana can be cultivated to become the breadbasket of the region, investment in agriculture is a major concern. It is not a new idea, but it is an idea whose time has come, and momentum is under way.

In anticipation of expanded revenues from oil, the government of Guyana has established a Sovereign Wealth Fund, known as the Natural Resources Fund (NRF). This is intended to capture royalties and other revenues from the oil and gas sector. The Fund will use natural resource wealth to finance national development priorities, including initiatives to realise an inclusive green economy. Eventually it also intends to have deposits of revenues from other extractive industries in Guyana. The fund incorporates a mix of short and long-term investments.

The government might also be encouraged to consider a Diaspora Investment Fund to attract investment from its citizens abroad. Once conditions are encouraging and processes for investment are smooth, the diaspora is a lucrative source of investment capital. This type of fund must develop clear strategies to attract international remittances. This has worked well in Kenya and other countries and in some cases it represents the largest source of foreign exchange for them.

Finally, there are investment opportunities in ecotourism. Guyana has a regional advantage given its holistic approach to sustainable destination management and development from its national policy for pursuing a Low Carbon Development Strategy (LCDS) as well as implementing a strategy and action plan based on sustainable tourism development.

Getting from here to there: Summary

Overall, investment in Guyana's future sustainability means making long-term investments in assets and people. Here is a summary of possible strategies:

- Guyana's forests have created environmental space for simultaneous development of its oil resources and its net carbon sink credentials;

- Put all Guyanese and Caribbean people first. All ethnic groups are equal in this trajectory;

- Do not inflate already enthusiastic domestic or regional public expectations;

- Be careful of strategies that try to do too much too quickly and tend to either fall short or fail;

- Choose carefully when using resources to solve infrastructural problems;

- Do not focus just on immediate problems but look at opportunities for the long term;

- Build global partnerships to advance the development of Guyana and CARICOM;

- Compete internationally with Guyana's cheap energy for industrial capacity in tandem with similar regional producers. In this context the 'Gas to Power' project for lowering electricity costs is a logical step;

- Invest heavily in agricultural business for the region. (Twenty-five per cent of CARICOM's food production can be met by Guyana.);

- Accelerate investment in traditional economic drivers such as mining and other extractive industries, multiplier businesses from the oil and gas industry, manufacturing, insurance, real estate, and other enterprises;

- Create new jobs in food processing, fertilizers, and petrochemicals; and

- Build strategies for low-carbon business models and articulate these strategies to markets.

Conclusion

The shape of our global energy systems is changing. Energy supply chains have altered significantly in the face of evolving market conditions, with new value chains emerging in ways previously unseen. New collaborative, circular partnerships, and new technologies such as hydrogen and carbon capture could alter the energy supply of the future. There is the risk in the global transitions that even top-flight oil producers such as Guyana could face the prospect of 'stranded assets' as trajectories to replace fossil fuels bear fruit. Guyana is in the driver's seat now in its progress toward becoming Oil Dorado.

About the contributor

Dr. Anthony T. Bryan is Professor Emeritus, the University of Miami, and a Professor/Senior Fellow of the Institute of International Relations at The University of the West Indies, St. Augustine Campus, Trinidad and Tobago, where he served as Professor/Director for a decade. He is a founding member of the Caribbean Policy Consortium based in Washington, D.C. and in Trinidad.

Chapter Nine

Plantation Houston EBD: The most valuable piece of real (sugar) estate in Guyana?

It is only 500 acres of former sugar estate, yet it is maybe worth billions of US dollars to one Guyanese family. How did Plantation Houston East Bank Demerara go from cane estate to black gold field? John Mair explains

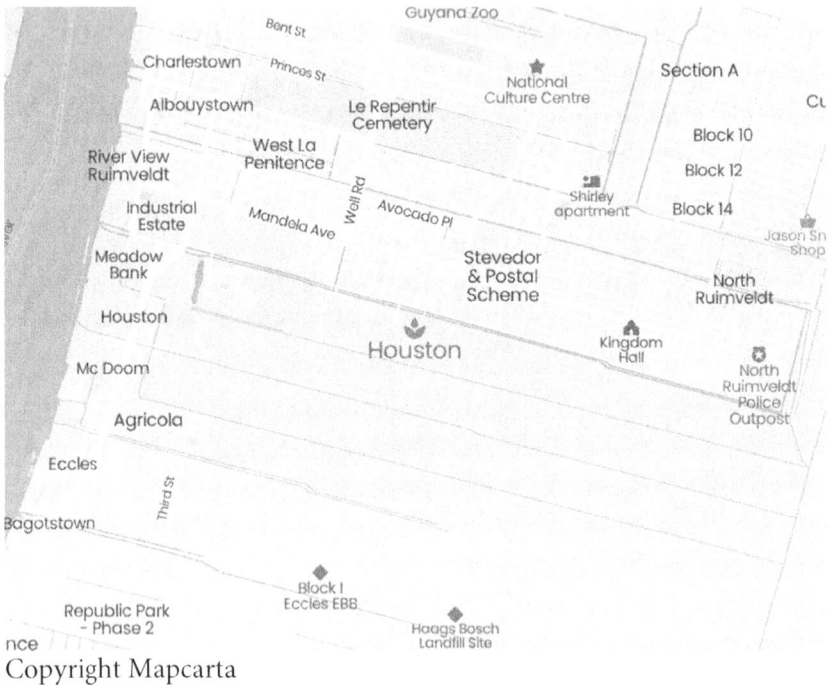

Copyright Mapcarta

Plantation Houston. East Bank Demerara. It was a small family sugar estate of 1,600 acres in the Georgetown suburbs producing insufficient cane to keep their own factory grinding. Today the 500 acres of former cane field still left in the Vieira family are, almost literally, a gold field.

How did those fields become such a money tree?

72

Shore Base Central

Today, Houston in Guyana is the epicentre of the oil bonanza, replete with shore supply bases for the deep-sea offshore oil industry, still mainly ExxonMobil. It is just six miles from the mouth of the Demerara River, situated before the barrier of the Demerara Harbour Bridge which, when built in 1976, was deemed the world's longest floating bridge (LFSB). Local wags turned the initialism to the Linden Forbes Sampson Bridge in ironic tribute to the dictator LFS Burnham whose prize project it was.

In 2023, the entire river frontage in Houston is occupied by big world names like Schlumberger and the (Guyanese-fronted) Guyana Shore Base Inc (GSYBI). They supply the offshore industry with provisions, assembly, repairs, and much more, and receive, in return, from the floating production offshore ships, their detritus, mud, and garbage of all sorts to turn it into something more environmentally acceptable.

The Houston River frontage is at a premium. GSYBI alone claims to have invested US$150m there in the last five years. GSYBI paid US$18m for eight acres in 2019. Today, their whole site is 170 acres. Their original waterfront has expanded to 32 acres plus some 104 acres across the main road -- the eastern side -- bought from the Vieira family and their Houston sugar estate.

Schlumberger next door occupies a similar space. To get to that size they have bought land from others. Some of their land was previously owned by a prominent Indo-Guyanese family the Rahamans. That was a timber facility: Caribbean Timbers. Land was also bought from a local Indo hardware baron, Sataur Gafoor, who moved his wholesale premises lock stock and barrel down the road. Ironically, he bought that land from Houston estate to re-site it. A wharf owned by Eddy Vieira was sold to Totaltec a Guyanese/American oil support company.

Houston Riverside is a modern version of Oil Monopoly.

It surely cannot be long before today's oil barons colonise the adjacent Demerara Sugar Terminal, the long-established export hub for the country's slow dying sugar industry.

The Vieira dynasty

How did the Vieiras come to be in this fortunate position? Family money, good husbandry, and happenstance. It was started by Manoel Senior who bought himself out of indentureship and set up a liquor business (in Guyanese parlance a rum shop) in Anna Caterina West Coast Demerara. It made money. Plenty. Enough to set up his family well.

Houston estate, the first to be owned in the 'colony' by a local Guyanese family, was bought in 1903 by Manoel Vieira Junior. He came from that old Portuguese/Guianese landed family.

After a spell in the liquor business, Manoel Junior went into the Guianese interior and prospected for diamonds with huge success.

Houston Plantation goes native

With the proceeds of that, Vieira bought Plantation Houston. His son Joseph Vieira, who was interested from an early age in agriculture, took over running the family estate in 1944 and, in time, he became one of the best and most profitable planters in 'BG'. His husbandry and profit-making skills were mellowed by Roman Catholic philanthropy learned from his Salesian education in the UK.

The family invested well and it bore results in the crops and more.

Joe Vieira was one of the great planters, full of ideas. But his estate's crops were not large enough to maintain its own grinding factory. That had to be closed in 1955. The sugar estate struggled on post-

Independence through hostility from Presidents Burnham and Hoyte.

Raw materials become increasingly expensive as they were bought on the black market. Their sugar had to be sold on the white market. Houston still turned a profit on that. Joe's skills kept the sugar business going until it became firmly unprofitable and was abandoned in 2010, five years after his death. The next generation lost interest in sugar. The family had gone through some very hard times. Some of the land in Houston had to be sold off to pay off debts to Banks Breweries and some to Guysuco in Versailles (another Vieira plantation).

Away from core sugar, some of the Vieiras went into riverside businesses. A small shipyard was established in 1981 as well as an allied machinery supply business plus a fish processing business.
Up to 2010, the sugar estate had continued in its area limited way. Their fields were right up against sprawling Georgetown and boxed in by new EBD communities like Eccles and McDoom. Their fertile land was eyed up by many for decades.

The proceeds from the non-sugar enterprises were small fry compared with the riches when the oil boom came calling from 2017 onwards.

Oil Dorado comes to Houston

The Vieira family got into that phenomenon early with sales of land on the eastern side of the public road that crossed their estate.

Real estate came calling too. In 2019, Houston Estate sold 52 acres for housing to Redstart Investments, a half Guyanese company. Today, those former fields are luxury condos. The drainage canal, vital to cane cultivation, was filled in during the same year. Cane sugar cultivation was firmly no more at Plantation Houston after a century and more. Oil Dorado was to be the Vieira family future.

A traveller in time, even from the recent past, would not recognise Houston today. The change in the last decade is immense: huge warehouses, ritzy blocks of flats, either built or planned with expensive rents of US$3,000-5,000 per month. From the air you can just see the green remains of the sugar estate fields on the eastern side of the shore bases. A new highway just being built from urban Georgetown to suburban Diamond -- with oil money -- cuts through the remnants of the Houston estate. That makes those 500 acres even more valuable.

But it has not been all plain sailing within the Vieira dynasty. Two cousins of the current family group, Houston residents Vanda and Danuta Radzik, took it upon themselves in 2022 to sue Schlumberger for storing radioactive material on their site, having, say the Radziks, railroaded through permission from the Environment Protection Agency without proper investigation. They won their case in the High Court in December 2022 and, for now, have put a stop to that.

Houston East Bank Demerara is a metaphor for the metamorphosis of Guyana from a mono-crop sugar economy, in colonial and post-colonial times, to the oil bonanza of the last five years. The big old Portuguese and Indian families like the Vieiras, the Fernandes, the Gafoors, and the Muneshwers saw that future and bought into it. Lock, stock, and oil barrel.

What happens to the last 500 acres of those former sugar cane fields is a portent for Guyana's future. Sugar is dead, oil is alive. It is unlikely that the Vieira dynasty will lose out.

Note on contributor

To declare interests, John Mair is a child of sugar. My father planted five miles down the East Bank Road from Houston on a British-owned estate in the 1950s. He managed Peter's Hall. I grew up there. I am also a long-standing personal friend of Anthony Vieira. He contributed to this piece.

Chapter Ten
On the brighter side of Oil Dorado

What if we believe in the 'One Guyana' initiative? Melissa Varswyk, CEO of the Georgetown American University, asks, Who wins?

Being an optimist, I often focus on positive thoughts. When I was asked to write about my hopes and fears of Oil Dorado Guyana, I did with enthusiasm, I kept the 'fear' at bay: I can only be sanguine about prospects for the future of Guyana and all Guyanese.

Patriotism

In 2005, over 100 Guyanese youths (including me) were sponsored by the government of Guyana to attend a youth conference in Caracas. I recall an incident where a group of Venezuelans asked the Guyanese delegation which country we were representing. Our response sparked an immediate reply, 'Essequibo'! Being patriotic Guyanese, knowing the border controversy between the two countries, we instantly replied, 'We Essequibo'!

In my experience, as much as Guyanese criticise the day-to-day matters of Guyana, we always defend and proclaim our native land. I believe every Guyanese has an experience where they felt patriotic regardless of how much Guyana has served (or not) in their best interests. And while the minimum opportunities for self-growth and development were not always equitably distributed, whether because of the scarcity of resources or just deliberate actions, I hope we can refer to that as in the past.

Oil Dorado has now created the scope for endless opportunities for the development of all Guyanese. I hope we can refer to this as our future. Now that Guyana is harvesting her wealth, the patriots who stood strong with her through good times and bad must reap rewards.

Guyanese first!

Guyanese must be first-class citizens in our country! I define first-class citizens as the dominant group of residents with access to all applicable opportunities without any deliberate hindrance. This is my hope, as many resource-rich developing countries have recorded a different path. In an official US publication it was noted that: '[U]nder the so-called African resource curse, African citizens don't benefit from these resources to the extent that would be expected. Education, health care, and other services are not provided to citizens' (US House Hearing, 113 Congress (2013)).

Guyana's NRF, its sovereign wealth fund, is expected to contribute to development in three main areas, health, education, and infrastructure. I hope that healthcare, education, and infrastructural development delivered in Aishalton in the Guyanese interior will be the same as in Georgetown, the Guyanese capital. We are heading in this direction with the thousands of scholarships allocated to Guyanese, the expansion of healthcare services, and infrastructure development throughout the country. As the government crafts the vision and policies for the development of Guyana, the agencies of government need to follow through with transparent and efficient implementation processes.

The Local Content Act, a work in progress, was created to secure endless opportunities for Guyanese and the development of Guyana. A recent incident has highlighted loopholes in that legislation, which propelled the local private sector to lobby for strengthening of the legislation. As long as the private sector continues to serve as the 'watchdog' for local content, Guyana stands a better chance of benefiting significantly from the emerging energy sector.

But we all have a duty

The focus is on the government and the private sector to aid the country's development, but we often forget the role and responsibilities of citizens. For this initiative to succeed, grassroots leaders need to ensure that the communities they serve have access to the available opportunities and to provide oversight of the quality of work and services provided to their people.

We are faced with a largely unskilled workforce. Moreover, there is an inevitable labour re-allocation towards the oil and gas sector. Increasing opportunities for quality education can become a significant step toward filling these gaps if most Guyanese have access.

There is no doubt there were not always equal opportunities for all in Guyana and that there is not currently a diverse economy. One of the contributing factors is the lack of access to financing and other resources that aid the transformative growth of small and medium-sized businesses.

I am constantly reminded of a meeting between my partner and a government minister that occurred a few years ago. He proposed to the minister that the government should consider creating an equipment pool for small contractors to have access to assist them in becoming eligible for bidding on contracts. The Minister responded with a blank stare.

The government is responsible for creating a level playing field to diversify the economy. This will contribute to growth throughout the length and breadth of Guyana among all communities, groups, and peoples. Again, the citizens of Guyana have a responsibility to prepare themselves for the windfall of opportunities for growth and development that come with oil wealth.

Guyana is developing at a fast pace, faster than many can envision at this time. The playing field will become more competitive than ever, and we must get our businesses in order, explore opportunities for partnerships, and be assertive toward meeting goals.

Where there is equal growth, there is likely to be stability.

Is it all good news?

The pessimists will see doom and gloom ahead for Guyana. If we live in the past and don't diversify the economy, they may win the debate. Guyana wins when community engagement, women at the decision-making table, equitable distribution of resources, and maintenance of a robust private sector become the status quo. This is not new. It is simply a fulfilment of our national motto 'One People, One Nation, One Destiny', acting on the sweet melodies of our nation.

Let us cooperate for Guyana. Let us cooperate for our land. Let us resolve to fight together. See, we do it right together. Can we do it? Yes, we can!

Reference

House Hearing, 113 Congress (2013) Is there an African Resource Curse? The US Government Publishing Office. Available at: https://www.govinfo.gov/content/pkg/CHRG-113hhrg81978/html/CHRG-113hhrg81978.htm Retrieved January 2, 2023.

About the Contributor

Dr. Melissa Varswyk is the Chief Executive Officer of Georgetown American University, established in Guyana and the USA. She graduated with a Doctor of Medicine Degree. She serves as the Vice-Chair of Women in Energy, the Black Entrepreneurs Association, and the Private Sector Commission Local Content Advisory Committee. She is also on the Board of Directors of the American Chamber of Commerce, Guyana. She has received several awards, including the Most Influential Person of African Descent under 40 and one of the 25 Most Influential Women Leaders in Guyana.

Chapter Eleven
Footing the bill for climate change impacts with petrodollars

The cost of national recovery after devastating floods and drought is often borne directly or indirectly by petrodollars. As activists call for a halt to oil production, UWI's Dr Lorraine Sobers argues Guyana has limited choices for funding its development while recovering from the impacts of climate change

Determining how much various countries pay for climate change impacts is complex. What is clear is the lack of correlation between the countries most affected by climate change, footing the bill to recover from climatic events, and those responsible for massive greenhouse gas emissions.

Guyana's position at the table

Guyana commenced production just two years ago, almost 150 years after the world's oil industry was established. Remarkably, Guyana's present oil production rate, approximately 300,000 barrels per day, is expected to quadruple by 2027 (Rystad Energy 2022). For many years Guyana has had the second-lowest gross domestic product (GDP) in the Caribbean, however, Professor Anthony Bryan (see chapter 11 of this book) predicts that revenue from petrodollars will amount to at least US$50bn and up to US$200bn within the next three decades. Guyana has gained international attention because of its large oil reserves, 11bn barrels so far, discovered in the offshore Stabroek Block (News Room 2022). This good fortune is tempered by energy markets moving away from fossil fuels toward renewable energy as the part of the global energy transition.

These large offshore oil discoveries place Guyana in a unique position. Typically, Small Island Developing States (SIDS) like Guyana have a low carbon footprint. However, these countries are most susceptible to the effects of climate change such as rising sea levels and changing rainfall patterns. Although Guyana is poised to take its place in the top sixteen international oil producers, it has long been a significant carbon sink with 18m hectares of forest, storing 19 gigatonnes of carbon dioxide (CO_2), removing over 154m tonnes of CO_2 annually (Office of the President 2022). Guyana's Low Carbon Developing Strategy 2030 (LCDS) outlines how the country intends to advance its development as an oil producer.

The Tyndall Centre report 'Phaseout Pathways for Fossil Fuel Production' proposes that, 'The poorest countries should be given until 2050 to end production, but they will also need significant financial support to transition their economies within that time frame [...] there is no practical emission space [...] for any nation to develop any new production facilities of any kind' (Calverley & Anderson 2022). However, it is not apparent exactly how Guyana will fund its LCDS and other national development priorities without internally or externally, directly or indirectly generated, petrodollars. African Petroleum Producers' Organization (APPO) Secretary General Omar Farouk Ibrahim clearly put forward the position of several developing countries: 'We will not allow billions of barrels of oil to go to waste and we will not be bamboozled into projects that we don't need – ones which will not address energy poverty. We need to sit down and have an honest conversation about the energy transition' (Ford 2021).

The Guyanese people are eager to modernise and expand the nation's infrastructure, education and healthcare facilities with its petrodollar windfall. However, energy experts believe that the income from oil production will begin to shrink as demand for fossil fuels declines after 2050. The path outlined by the LCDS includes these improvements alongside forest climate services, the low-carbon energy transition, protection against climate change, and management of the oil and gas industry. So far, the strategy seems destined to be funded by petrodollars from Guyana, oil-producing countries and energy companies.

Who is currently paying for climate change impacts?

Between 1997 and 2016 Guyana experienced significant flooding events in eight of those years and drought in four. The scale of flooding damage in a single year, 2005, was estimated to be 60 per cent of the country's GDP at that time. It is glaringly obvious that such regular, crippling setbacks can only be addressed by large injections of funds (Office of the President 2022). The Guyana National Resource Fund established in 2021is a sovereign wealth fund that is an accumulation of windfall revenue from oil production. Withdrawals from this fund are allowed for 'national development priorities' and 'ameliorating the effects of national disasters' (Parliament of Guyana 2021). The national disasters usually experienced by Guyana are climatic events, flood and drought, attributed to climate change. So, in fact, petrodollars are being put aside deal with climate change impacts.

In 2009, oil-rich Norway purchased US$250m in carbon credits from Guyana under the United Nations Reducing Emissions from Deforestation and Forest Degradation programme (REDD+) (Office of the President 2022). The recent purchase of US$750m in carbon credit by Hess Corporation (2022), a consortium partner in Guyana's offshore oil sector, from the Government of Guyana is likely to be directed, in part, to the objectives of the LCDS including combating climate change.

The United Nations established the United Nations Framework Convention on Climate Change (UNFCCC) under which industrialized nations agree to 'support climate change activities in developing countries by providing financial support for action on climate change'. Industrialised nations, identified under Annex I of the Kyoto Protocol, agree to foot the bill for climate change. This, among other pertinent objectives, has been on the agenda of 27 annual meetings of parties to this framework convention known as Conference of the Parties (COP).

The UNFCCC presented studies that show industrialised nations to be major sources of past and current greenhouse gas emissions attributed to climate change. Based on these studies and their recommendations, signatories to the Kyoto Protocol undertake to bear the responsibility of cutting their emissions and funding mitigation and adaptation activities of developing countries

(UNFCCC 1997). Arguably, pledges to fund these activities have not materialised as far-reaching, effective relief. Further, this did not address the burden of recovery cost carried by SIDS. Several reports have found that the volume of funding becomes somewhat diminished as it moves from donor agency to having an impact on the average Caribbean citizen experiencing the aftermath of a devastating hurricane or flood.

After decades of advocacy for 'loss and damage' funding, the efforts of SIDS have advanced with the agreement made at the COP27 to fund recovery costs (UNFCCC 2022). This response recalls the 2022 Bridgetown Initiative (Ministry of Foreign Affairs 2022) asking for 'a global mechanism for raising reconstruction grants for any country just imperilled by a climate disaster. And […] new issuance of US$650bn or other low-interest, long-term instruments to back a multilateral agency that accelerates private investment in the low carbon transition, wherever it is most effective'.

The energy transition

Undeniably, this low-carbon transition, also known as the energy transition, is also part of the climate change cost. Developing countries are rich in renewable sources of energy such as solar, wind, hydro power etc, but the technology to harness these sources of energy is owned by and manufactured in developed countries. Funding, aid, tax incentives, and tax exemptions are often redirected back to developed countries through the purchase of equipment, goods and services (Thomas et al 2019). Bear in mind that oil and gas companies, rebranded as energy companies, have also invested in the research and development of renewable energy technology. Developing countries need to carefully consider how they engage in trade and procurement under the umbrella of low-carbon development.

The energy transition means a movement from fossil fuels to renewable energy. Dr. Devon Gardner of the Caribbean Centre for Renewable Energy and Energy Efficiency (CCREEE) has noted the challenge of financing renewable energy projects in the Caribbean, stating, 'many countries have not been able to find appropriate financing modality to bring these projects to bear' (Sobers 2022). However, the newly oil-rich Guyana intends to use a mix of natural gas, a fossil fuel, alongside renewable energy sources, solar and hydropower energy, in its LCDS. Guyana's petrodollars will be used to transition its power generation to cleaner and greener energy. The power generation sector plans to switch from fuel oil (FO) imports to using natural gas from offshore reservoirs. Although natural gas is a fossil fuel, it produces 50 per cent less greenhouse gas than fuel oil. Natural gas has been characterised as a 'bridge' to the ultimate destination of green energy (Office of the President 2022), however, this will only be realized if there is a more aggressive approach to establishing a decentralised renewable power generation network with built-in redundancy.

Guyana holds a unique position in being a long-standing significant carbon sink, swiftly becoming a significant oil producer, and now set to rapidly transition to cleaner energy while developing a poor nation in less than a decade. The country will need every petrodollar it earns to face the future.

References

Dan Calverley and Kevin Anderson (2022) 'Phaseout Pathways for Fossil Fuel Production within Paris-Compliant Carbon Budgets', 22 March, p. 76.

Neil Ford (2021) 'Africa Walks Development Tightrope as Calls for Oil and Gas Restraint Grow 'African Business, 31 October. Available online at https://african.business/2021/10/energy-resources/africa-walks-development-tightrope-as-calls-for-oil-and-gas-restraint-grow/, accessed 31 December 2022

Hess Corporation (2022) 'Hess Corporation and the Government of Guyana Announce Redd+ Carbon Credits Purchase Agreement', 2 December. Available online at https://investors.hess.com/news-releases/news-release-details/hess-corporation-and-government-guyana-announce-redd-carbon, accessed 31 December 2022

Ministry of Foreign Affairs and Foreign Trade, Barbados (2022) 'Urgent and Decisive Action Required for an Unprecedented Combination of Crises the 2022 Bridgetown Agenda for the Reform of the Global Financial Architecture, The 2022 Bridgetown Initiative', 23 September. Available online at https://www.foreign.gov.bb/the-2022-barbados-agenda/, accessed on 31 December 2022

News Room (2022) Guyana Could Earn US$200bn from Oil by 2050- Energy Expert, News Room. Available online at https://newsroom.gy/2022/05/16/guyana-could-earn-us200b-from-oil-by-2050-energy-expert/ , accessed 31 December 2022

Office of the President, Guyana 'Guyana's Low Carbon Development Strategy 2030' July 2022. Available online at https://lcds.gov.gy/wp-content/uploads/2022/08/Guyanas-Low-Carbon-Development-Strategy-2030.pdf1, accessed 31 December 2022

Parliament of Guyana (2021) 'Natural Resource Fund Act 2021' Act No. 19 of 2021

Rystad Energy (2022) Report 'Guyana Upstream Industry and Country Benchmarking Update' Rystad Energy, 21 July. Available online at https://research.manchester.ac.uk/en/publications/phaseout-pathways-for-fossil-fuel-production-within-paris-complia, accessed 31 December 2022

Lorraine Sobers (2022) 'A Sustainable Energy System for Guyana' OilNOW, 2 March. Available online at https://oilnow.gy/featured/a-sustainable-energy-system-for-guyana/, accessed 31 December 2022

Adelle Thomas, et al. 'Climate Change Adaptation Planning in Practice: Insights from the Caribbean', Regional Environmental Change, Vol. 19, No. 7, pp. 2013-2025.

UNFCCC (1997) 'Kyoto Protocol to the United Nations Framework Convention on Climate Change' 10 December.

UNFCCC (2021) Sessional Proceedings—'Sharm El-Sheikh Implementation Plan' Sharm el-Sheikh Climate Change Conference-November 2022, 20 November

About the contributor

Dr. Lorraine Sobers is a Fulbright Scholar and SPE Certified Engineer currently lecturing at the University of the West Indies, St. Augustine. Dr Sobers has a BSc in Chemical Engineering, an MS in Petroleum Engineering from Texas Tech, and a PhD in Petroleum Engineering from Imperial College, London. She has 20 years experience in the energy sector specialising in Carbon Capture and Storage (CCS). Dr. Sobers is the Project Coordinator for CO_2 Emission Reduction MobiLization (CERM) Project, and a Fellow of the Caribbean Policy Consortium.

Chapter Twelve

Will oil wealth trickle down to benefit ordinary Guyanese?

Narissa Deokarran lives in Lusignan, in the Guyanese countryside away from the oil bubble of Georgetown and offshore Guyana. Here she makes a plea from the streets and back dams to use the oil windfall to help the people of Guyana

Since the discovery of billions of barrels of oil in Guyana, the development prospects for the country have never been rosier. Guyana has suddenly become the place to be for international conglomerates, whether in oil and gas, tourism, food and beverage, or any other area that forecasters have deemed to be gold mines.

However, not everyone sees the oil discovery as a gift from the gods. Some see it as a harbinger of worse woes. While these individuals have valid concerns, especially those related to the environment, terms of contract, and benefits for the locals, oil wealth has the power to transform the country for the better if managed properly. For decades, this developing country has been plagued by one of the highest rates of emigration and brain drain, poor infrastructure, a high poverty rate, corruption, and mismanagement. However, the developmental transformation that might happen could make Guyana a country that her citizens want to live in and help build rather than flee from but there's a long winding road ahead to traverse before we get to that point.

How we live today

While the big local businesses, wealthy individuals, and international investors are seeing increased profits and/or opportunities, the vast majority of Guyana's population, with little disposable income but hopes for a better standard of living, wonder when their turn to benefit from being citizens of the much hyped 'fastest-growing economy in the world' will come.

The Government of Guyana is seen as pro-capitalist and investment-friendly. And it has consistently doled out enticing gifts to the private sector and sounded the call for entrepreneurship and investment. Although well intentioned and necessary for economic growth and development, most Guyanese lack the funds and/or skills needed to launch their own initiatives. Then again, when one considers other factors such as competition, the failure rate of new business ventures, lack of job security, and difficulties with sourcing funds to launch and continue one's operation, entrepreneurship may not seem so attractive from the get-go.

How can people improve their standard of living if the reality for the majority is low wages with little disposable income? And even if Guyanese are 'fortunate' to land jobs in the oil industry these are usually at entry level because they lack the specialised knowledge and skills to function effectively in the more technical, higher-paying positions.

Education, education, education

One way the oil wealth can benefit Guyanese is by focusing and spending more on the education sector and by extension providing better facilities, more opportunities opened to the public to further their education, increased programme choices and flexibility with timings at the tertiary level, and free education from nursery to university. With a population of under one million, this is doable and much needed and chimes with the often quoted but very true maxim 'Give a man a fish and he will eat for a day. Teach a man how to fish and you feed him for a lifetime'.

Education provides a pathway for people to improve their quality of life. Not only would they be in receipt of better salaries or equipped with the knowledge and skills to set up their own business/venture but society benefits when social ills linked to unemployment decrease. In addition, generational wealth is created through economic upliftment; this gives descendants greater opportunities to improve their own lives and contribute meaningfully to society.

Poor education; my nightmares

However, at this moment there is much to be done regarding the quality and access to education in Guyana. Many schools are in need of renovation, equipment, furniture, or simply require repurposing because they can no longer function effectively as schools.

For instance, I taught at Ann's Grove Secondary School which had an enrolment of over 500 students, yet there wasn't enough space in the yard for the teenage children to play in. During recess the children 'played' near the toilets. The school was just an open space without walls separating the classes. This led to students being easily distracted by the activities in nearby classes. Poor performance overall was the norm rather than the exception. In addition, there was no staff room, and so teachers had to find and claim an unoccupied spot in a corner with their marked chair and table. If one didn't write one's name on the chair and table, the chance of it being 'stolen' by another teacher was very high.

At another school at which I taught, Annandale Secondary School, the teachers have been sitting permanently in the library for years because the staff room is crammed. Thus students cannot use the library effectively and teachers are confined to an ill-suited and poorly ventilated environment. Although education officials visit regularly and the administrative staff is aware of the problem, nothing has been done to repurpose unused sections of the building into another staff room or to extend existing provision.

Here you have two schools with issues affecting both teachers and students that can be easily addressed, yet there is the lack of will to act and make decisions by those in authority that would bring about positive change. This is a microcosm of Guyana: the decision makers act independently, yet they lack vision.

Even the University of Guyana has fallen short in meeting the needs of prospective and current students from a wider cross-section of the population. Although most of the students come from working-class backgrounds the university itself remains elitist. This has forced many young people to either drop out from their programme or to switch to ones with less attractive career prospects. For instance, most STEM programmes can only be done full-time. Therefore one must be financially supported by relatives. Due to this, the programmes attract the fewest students and the developmental need for skilled persons in these areas remain unfulfilled.

Great wealth but poor people

For decades Guyana's growth remained stagnant and the dreams of many were to leave these shores for greener pastures. However, with its new-found wealth the citizens of the land should be the ones reaping the most benefits through jobs or other opportunities. Although the manpower needs of an economy experiencing rapid growth may not be fully met through local labour, Guyanese should not be just entry-level workers without hopes of climbing the ladder in these companies making billions of US dollars from the resources that are present in Guyana.

Apart from the government's responsibility to the citizens of the country, foreign companies operating here also have a responsibility to the people. Through training opportunities, scholarships, and mentoring Guyanese should be able to fill key positions in the near future in these companies.

At the moment, though, many cannot envision the transformation that can be had because all are feeling the squeeze economically from high inflation fuelled partly by the rosy economic prospects that pundits have foretold. But because of meagre salaries the spending power of the masses have decreased, and they find themselves poorer. While there are naysayers isolated in their ivory towers and oblivious to the plight of the ordinary person, a quick trip to any market would prove to be an eye-opening experience. The prices of many locally produced vegetables and other commodities have risen by 100 per cent and more. For example, I visit the Mon Repos market once a week and it is astonishing to witness by how much the prices of local vegetables have risen; a pound of shallots that not so long ago was GY$200–300 (US1-1.50) is now over $1,000; a pound of celery now costs GY$3,000 from selling for less than GY$500; and a parcel of boulanger has moved from selling for GY$200 to GY$500 and so on. In addition, the price of buying houses and the cost of renting have also increased significantly because owners and landlords can sell and rent at a higher price to the foreigners and overseas-based Guyanese with deeper pockets.

A house lot for all? There is room for improvement

While the Government has put in place measures to ensure that Guyanese are able to access residential land at affordable prices, the process can be improved. Why is there a waiting period of over a decade or two for some while others are able to secure theirs in a year or two? And why is the Ministry of Housing calling persons after their decade of waiting to pull numbers and sign an Agreement of Sale for areas that are undeveloped? It would be better to allocate persons land in areas already prepared so that the process of building can begin, and homeowners could enjoy some good years in their houses before the inevitable call to the beyond occurs. The entire process of allocating house lots needs to be more transparent, equitable, and timely.

Then again, when the ordinary Guyanese is allocated a plot of land at an affordable price, a new issue of gigantic proportions arises: how and where to secure funds from to start the building process? Many plots are left bare for years because of this issue. Most Guyanese whose work is vital but salaries meagre need to be paid liveable wages and oil funds will aid this. While the process has begun, it need not be in a haphazard manner and seen as handouts being given out by 'Santa' at Christmas time. After all, the resources of the land belong to all Guyanese and receiving the benefits from these should be dignified and not like kneeling with a begging bowl in outstretched hands.

My dream

The time to benefit is now and the oil wealth currently flowing in has the potential to transform the lives of citizens for the better. With good governance and management of state resources Guyana can truly be Oil Dorado!

About the contributor

Narissa Deokarran is a blogger who focuses mainly on issues related to women's empowerment, the environment, her community and country as a whole. She won a Clare Forrester PAHO/WHO media award for excellence in Health Journalism. She is a contributing author to V.S. Naipaul: The Legacy edited by John Mair, Richard Lance Keeble, and Farrukh Dhondy.

Chapter Thirteen

Guyana's oil boom budget: The view from Trinidad and Tobago

How was the January 2023 Guyana budget seen from Trinidad and Tobago? Mark Wilson reports on Guyana's oil-fuelled economic boom, and reflects on a situation where, while Guyana pumps oil, the world is experiencing a climate crisis

Monday 16 January 2023 was budget day in Guyana, finance minister Ashni Singh plans to spend 41 per cent more than he did in 2022. He can afford to. He has a US$1bn transfer from Guyana's Natural Resource Fund to play with. Tax revenues are up. On top of that, he's planning a budget deficit equivalent to 11.5 per cent of Guyana's soaring economic output. And at the start of the year, he announced US$364m Chinese borrowing to pay for a new bridge over the Demerara River and an East Coast highway.

Singh increased pensions by 18 per cent. Public servants have just had an eight per cent pay increase. Though it's still under TT$2,000 a month (US$293.60) the private sector minimum wage went up 36 per cent in July 2022. Tax on gas and diesel has been cut to zero.

Not just oil

Guyana's economy was the world's fastest growing in 2022, with output up 62 per cent. And it's not just oil. The non-oil economy was up by 12 per cent. Bauxite is rebounding. Gold prices are peaking again. diamonds are sparkling. There's a new manganese mine. And the government has spent US$50m in two years trying to revive the moribund sugar industry, with another US$20m to follow in 2023.

Construction boomed by 26 per cent. Says one city dweller: "Georgetown is one big construction site." There's talk of importing aggregate from Canada. Cement importers sell stock faster than they can reorder. Plumbers and electricians charge a hefty 'consultation fee' to even look at a job. And traffic? Wall-to-wall SUVs block the Georgetown roads.

When I first went to Guyana in the mid-1980s, basic foods like cheese, potatoes or what flour were unobtainable. A scatter of ancient Austin and Morris taxis sputtered the roads. Guyanese hunted every possible route to work overseas.

A glitzy Georgetown restaurant now does a brisk trade in steaks at TT$2,250 (US$33030) a throw. Champagne sales are bubbling.

Not everyone is laughing though. Vegetable prices doubled last year; eggs are up almost as much. Stabroek News publishes heart-wrenchingly weekly vox-pop features highlighting the struggles of the rural and urban poor.

From a standing start in 2020, oil output reached 233,000 barrels a day in December 2022, with 560,000 expected by December 2023. That would be around ten times Trinidad and Tobago's output. By 2027, ExxonMobil and partners expect to reach 1.2m daily barrels. Reserves are now over 11bn barrels, with new finds still stacking up, and a bid round closing in April 2023. There's 17tn cubic feet of gas, earmarked for a new power plant to fix Guyana's ongoing power supply woes. A small oil refinery is proposed, for completion in 2025.

Trinidad and Tobago businesses such as Ansa McAL, Massy, and Republic Bank are poised to share Guyana's prosperity. So are a clutch of smaller energy sector enterprises.

In a few more years, will we have a Caribbean Dubai or Abu Dhabi? Even allowing for leakages to waste and corruption, there will be plenty cash for the useful stuff.

While Guyana pumps oil, the world is in climate crisis.

Guyana's climate crisis

The big threat to Guyana is steadily rising sea levels. Most Guyanese live in the coastal strip, at or below high tide. Critical sea defences are already at risk. By July 2023, the US gives a 64 per cent chance of an El Niño weather pattern. That means searing drought for Guyana. This follows three years of heavy rain and flooding from the inverse La Niña pattern. An unstable worldwide climate is making these swings sharper and more damaging. Drought and deforestation have pushed Amazonian and Guyanese rain forests close to an environmentally disastrous tipping point.

Guyana's ultra-influential vice president Bharrat Jagdeo was executive president from 1999 to 2011. In 2009 he announced a Low Carbon Development Strategy, to include international payments for the carbon-absorbing impact of forest conservation. An updated version launched last year also takes in biodiversity conservation, fresh water, and the ocean economy. That requires careful management.

Guyana was given 3.5m carbon credits last year for not cutting down its trees, with more to come. In December 2022 ExxonMobil's offshore partner Hess agreed to buy one third of these credits, paying US$750m over ten years. fifteen per cent of those funds will go to Village Sustainability Plans for Amerindian settlements in the forested interior.

With construction booming, Guyanese forest exploitation for timber grew 13 per cent last year. The government hopes it will increase further with the first stage of a new road to Brazil easing forest access. Internationally, research published in January 2023 strongly questions the validity of many forest conservation carbon offsets.

Recently unearthed documents show that Exxon's scientists accurately predicted the impact of oil extraction on the world's climate as early as the 1970s. on Tuesday 17 January, on the second day of the World Economic Forum at Davos, UN General Secretary António Guterres said that, "Fossil fuel producers and their enablers are still racing to expand production, knowing full well that their business model is inconsistent with human survival. This insanity belongs in science fiction."

After centuries of hardship, it's hard to begrudge the Guyanese their oil boom. In Trinidad and Tobago, we're familiar with the upsides and downsides. Yes, it's a development strategy.

But Low Carbon? Maybe not.

A version of this chapter first appeared in the Trinidad Express.

About the contributor

Based in Port of Spain, Mark Wilson is a writer and researcher specialising in Caribbean affairs.

SECTION TWO: DISCORD IN PARADISE

Introduction
John Mair

In Oil Dorado not all the waters offshore and onshore are still. Not everybody is jumping up and down with joy at the idea of an oil bonanza. There is a hard core, a strong element of dissenters. Many of them are settled abroad in the large Guyanese diaspora, especially the ones in North America. They throw intellectual hand grenades southwards. One such is Canada-based Dr Janette Bulkan. In her chapter "Is we turn now': The carousel of political power in Guyana' she argues that politics in Guyana is a racial merry-go-round. Who wins the elections, wins the spoils. With oil, those are huge.

Inside Guyana too there is a seam of dissent. I examine one rich seam in 'The Moray House Mensheviks'. This looks at the groups and people based around the talk shop that is Moray House, the former home of a great Guyanese newspaper editor David de Caires. The 'discussions' put on there are almost universally critical of the oil status quo.

Likewise GHK Lall, a Wall Street Banker turned Guyanese returnee, who very pointedly tries to puncture a few myths in his extremely well written weekly columns in The Kaieteur News. In 'Is it Guyana's time?' he urges caution but also hope. He concludes, 'The evolution of Guyana through its oil wealth is nothing less than a revolution; may it be a golden one. It is a beautiful story, one that has all the elements to be among the great ones told.'

A main witness at Moray House is often the irascible Christopher Ram, accountant, attorney, and the closest Guyana gets to a forensic analyst. He is an iconoclast. A sage and sceptic on the oil industry. Week after week in his column 'Every Man, Woman and Child in Guyana Must Become Oil-Minded', in the Stabroek News, he has poured cold water on troubled oil. In his chapter titled 'A new age dawns, finally', he draws a positive conclusion: 'The clues were there but it has taken decades of hope – and border disputes – for oil to be finally realised'. Since 2019, Ram's cynicism has hardened. Week after week he is a critic.

Finally, on a definitely positive note, Neil Passmore of Hannam and Partners, a frequent visitor to Guyana and now a long-time investor, explains 'Why I've invested in Oil Dorado'. He's put his money where his mouth is -- into coconuts and their oil not into offshore crude oil.

There is absolutely nothing wrong with active debates in Oil Dorado: the Guyanese love a good loud row. Whether the cacophony of discord in Guyana and abroad has any effect is firmly open to question.

Chapter Fourteen

'Is we turn now': The carousel of political power in Guyana (2022)

Politics is about power, nowhere more so than in newly oil-rich states like Guyana. But what happens when political state power comes across multi-national economic power 'Big Oil'. Is it a meeting of equals? Who are the masters now? Guyanese political scientist Dr Janette Bulkan discusses these burning questions

The first edition of *Oil Dorado?*, published in 2019, with a second edition in 2020, had contributions which range from Pollyanna-ish optimism to sober appraisal of the stagnant, indeed toxic, political system in Guyana. The inability of two political administrations (APNU+AFC in 2015-2020, PPP 2020-?) to get to grips with the high capitalist reality of Big Oil has meant that poor Guyanese get poorer while a few rich Guyanese are becoming hugely richer from the spinoffs from the efficient exploitation by ExxonMobil (XOM)1 of the deep-water oilfields discovered during 2012- 2015. Families who owned ocean-side land are selling out to international hotel chains, local entrepreneurs with river-side properties are selling out to petroleum shore base companies, and the well-connected are being awarded or enabled to acquire government-owned land in such locations as sure-fire investment opportunities. Vice-president Bharatt Jagdeo considers that the circumstantial evidence indicates that XOM and oil patch insiders knew ofthe initial discoveries well before they were publicly announced, beginningin May 2015. The evidence includes the scramble in the months before the national elections in May 2015 for petroleum concessions (exploration licences), including by Guyanese business people well connected to the PPP political party (an unbroken governing regime during 1992-2015), many having no known experience of petroleum exploration or production.[2] Wehave also the oral admission in November 2021 by XOM's preferred environmental consultancy ERM that initial work on Guyana was begun in 2014.[3]? This prior knowledge in circulation makes the globally-worst Petroleum Sharing Agreement

(PSA) between XOM and Guyana signed in June 2016 all the more an indictment of the greedy despotism of the APNU+AFC Coalition government. It is widely believed in Guyana – and backed by a samizdat text – that XOM dictated favourable amendments to the generic PSA wording held by the Guyana Geology and Mines Commission (GGMC)and shared with XOM in 2012. It remains a matter of speculation why five Guyanese cabinet ministers were invited without technical support to XOMHQ in Texas in May 2016 and why the lead minister for natural resources and the environment, Raphael Trotman, signed the PSA a month later, apparently at the direction of the cabinet which contained five lawyers including himself; and why a second visit also by five cabinet ministers to the same XOM HQ in 2017 was followed by signature of the Petroleum Production Licence (PPL).

Some aspects of the discussions between Guyana and XOM are revealed in a report commissioned by the Government of Guyana from an independent agency, Clyde & Co., but details are believedto be buried in annexes which are not in the public domain (Kaieteur News 2021a).

The PSA 2016 was not published until 17 months after signature, but the PPL remain unpublished to this day. Both the PNC and PPP political parties, while in opposition, had promised to release all foreign direct investment (FDI) contracts or agreements, and Guyana is so required as a full member of the Norway-based Extractive Industries Transparency Initiative (EITI). However, no political administration in Guyana has released any of the FDI agreements for timber logging or mineral mining, and several petroleum documents remain unpublished.

How much oil offshore Guyana?

The United States Geological Survey's (USGS) World Petroleum Assessment 2000 indicated a possible resource of 13.6bn barrels (boe) and 20-30+ trillion cubic feet of associated gas (Donovan 2004: 669). USGS described it as the second most prospective, underexplored offshore oil basin in the world (OilNOW 2017). This favourable prognostication seems to have stimulated (or perhaps based partly on) a new wave of 3-D and 4-D seismic surveys by XOM, reviving activity in the huge Stabroek tract concession which had been covered by a prospection licence issued by Guyana in June 1999, modified by a little-known but accessible bridging deed in 2008.

At the time of finalising the PSA in June 2016, a second bridging deed (accessible with some difficulty in the public domain) and a currently inaccessible accompanying escrow letter held by a designated escrow agent ensured that all the rights held by XOM under the 1999 petroleum prospecting licence were carried over into the period of the PSA, in effect setting aside the legal requirements under the Petroleum (Exploration & Production) Act 1986 for relinquishment. The USGS forecast did not apparently cause any political or technical move in Guyana to modernise the legal context within which petroleum developments would operate. Whatever discussions took place between GGMC and the petroleum companies during 2012-15 and, indeed, until today (November 2021), have been framed by the Petroleum (Exploration & Production) Act 1986 (cap.65-10, PEPA) and the subsidiary regulations published at the same time in July 1986 (Datadin 2020). There is also a revision of PEPA with the same title but a different chapter number in the laws of Guyana (65-04) with a date 1997, of uncertain legal status.

Quis custodiet Big Oil?

As Sanjeev Datadin pointed out in a previous edition of *Oil Dorado?* the governmental structures for supervising and monitoring the oil and gas sector are multiple and apparently overlapping as well as in flux. In the past, the technical agency was the GGMC, whose Petroleum Division was expected in 2017 to transform into a new regulatory Petroleum Commission with a mandate 'to monitor and regulate the efficient, safe, effective and environmentally responsible exploration, development and production of petroleum' (Department of Public Information 2019). This commission was created but the enabling Petroleum Commission Bill, passed in

January 2019by the APNU+AFC Coalition while the opposition PPP had absented itself from the National Assembly and the Coalition government had caretaker status, was abandoned when the PPP resumed office in August 2020. The relevant GGMC staff have reverted to being a Petroleum Department. For taxation in relation to petroleum, the Guyana Revenue Authority (GRA)obtained advice from the International Monetary Fund (IMF) in a Guyana Technical Assistance Customs Petroleum Report (September 2019). The GRA established the Customs Petroleum Unit and Petroleum Revenue Audit Unit to focus on oil and gas audits and routine customs functions relevant to the sector.

The 'unit is overseen by a deputy commissioner and a staff complement that includes specialists in oil lifting and export, entry processing, classification and import valuation, data analysis and research, and exemption and inventory monitoring'.[4]

This GRA statement shows that, in principle, Guyana created the capacity to monitor petroleum production and check the tax liabilities in XOM's declared costs. There is acontradiction between this 2019 GRA statement and the Jagdeo statement in November 2021 that auditing of XOM costs could not be done (Kaieteur News 2021c).

Who audits the oil barons?

The PSA signed in 2016 allowed Guyana only two years to audit the XOM accounts for the validity of claims for tax exemptions. This limitation includes the accounts of pre-production costs and does not ring-fence accounts to individual oil fields. XOM can, therefore, mix costs associated with dry wells with those of productive wells, dry fields with productive fields, in order to minimise its overall tax liabilities. Urged by donor countries, the international finance agencies and the independent daily press to audit the XOM accounts for tax liabilities (Guyana Times 2021), the government contracted IHS Markit in or before December 2019 to work with the GGMC and GRA (iNews Guyana 2019). It is not clear what has happened to that audit report. A preliminary version was reviewed in Guyana, revised by IHS Markit and returned to the government. It is not clear if EEPGL has been engaged directly. By November 2021, Vice-president Bharrat Jagdeo announced that the audit had not been completed within the PSA-allowed two-year window and so Guyana is obliged to accept all of the tax liability claims by XOM – US$10bn charged to 'cost oil', an amount more than five times the national budget of Guyana.

Protests in the independent press against this dereliction of government responsibility (Kaieteur News 2021d) have produced no signs of contrition.

Does the state rule the oil roost?

Political oversight and direction was provided by the Ministry of Natural Resources (MNR) until February 2018, when responsibility was moved to the Ministry of the Presidency (MOTP) with a newly-created Department of Energy in the MOTP in August 2018.5 At the change of government in August 2020, from the APNU+AFC Coalition to the PPP, the Department of Energy vanished and control appeared to transfer to vice-president (VP) Jagdeo whose mandate is 'to provide objective, administrative and technical support to the constitutional functions of the parliament of Guyana and the people of Guyana'.6 There is also a separate minister of natural resources Vickram Bharrat. His independence from the VP is the subject of much discussion in Guyana. It is not clear how the GGMC's Petroleum Department relates to vice-president Jagdeo who makes almost all the government's public statements about this sector in his regular press briefings.

By 29 March 2017, the APNU+AFC Coalition government had at least begun to draft new legislation and to update existing legislation to govern the oil and gas sector, a draft Sovereign Wealth Fund Bill called in Guyanathe Natural Resources Fund (GNRF) was circulated for public consultationand MNR had 'already completed a review aimed at updating the PetroleumExploration and Production Act of 1986. Additionally, the draft LCRP – Local Content Requirements Policy – will be made available to the public by the end of this month'

(Government Information News Agency 2017). Both the GNRF and LCRP are mired in the perennial conflict between international best practices and local politico-business practices.

Following the May 2015 publication of and the discovery of the Liza oil fields, various international agencies have offered to assist Guyana in updating and expanding the legal framework and in capacity building of legal staff. These agencies have included the Inter-American Development Bank and World Bank, the Commonwealth Secretariat and the Royal Institution for International Affairs (Chatham House, UK), the governments of Canada, Ghana, India, Mexico, Trinidad and Tobago, UK and USA – and the Natural Resource Governance Institute (NRGI), New York. It is remarkable that, in the six years since the discovery of commercial oil in 2015, only the contested Guyana Natural Resources Fund Act has passed into law while other legislative and policy and institutional developments remain in various states of desultory development. These pending developments include insurance against ecosystem/environmental damage; local content and value addition policy framework; a Petroleum Commission Bill; revision of PEPA; and a proposal for an Oil Pollution Act.

Is Guyana an easy touch?

It would not be unfair to conclude by saying that the weak state of legislation, monitoring and government supervision of the petroleum sector in Guyana is enormously beneficial to the oil field concession holders and operators and their shareholders. Guyana has abundant sweet light crude, low operating costs (break-even US$25-35/barrel), almost no environmental controls or monitoring and pays all the enterprises' taxes.

Steve Coll's book on XOM's global commercial empire (Coll 2012) could have been written from Guyana's experience; that is, Guyana's technical and political decision-makers appear to have learned almost nothing from the previous experiences of other poor countries where commercial petroleum has been discovered. Unless there is a very visible legal error to be corrected (for example, the 25-

year environmental authorisation for the Liza-1 field inthe Stabroek tract, instead of the legally permitted five years), XOM has been allowed or actively encouraged to 'drill, baby, drill' as fast as possible (Wilburg 2021).

It is not that the one-sided PSA from 2016 has passed without comment afterits late disclosure. A serious and penetrating clause-by-clause dissection by accountant/lawyer Christopher Ram was undertaken in a series of more than90 columns in the independent Stabroek News under the title 'The Road to First Oil – Every Man, Woman and Child must become Oil-Minded', beginning in May 2017. Neither the APNU+AFC Coalition government during 2017-2020 nor the returning PPP government from August 2020 have taken advantage of his analysis to negotiate a less one-sided PSA, contrary to their expressed intentions while in opposition.

Why should we care?

It may be difficult for non-Guyanese to understand why the successive governments have been and are so subservient to XOM and other petroleum explorers, when they are the sovereign owners of the resource and there areabundant lessons and sources of advice about negotiating contracts. Unabashedly, two Ministers, who each twice visited ExxonMobil's HQ in Texas, insisted that there had been no negotiations: 'There was no formal negotiation process […] there was no obligation on the part of the company to enter into any negotiations with our government' (Gaskin 2018). There isa clue in the independent statements by three of the five cabinet ministers who were entertained at XOM HQ in May 2016. 'There is no paper trail of negotiations – Trotman tells Parliamentary Committee' (Rockcliffe-Campbell 2018). Why?

I suggest that we are clear that for the inexperienced and untrained Ministers appointed as rewards for loyalty to the party leaders, petroleum appeared tobe no different from other natural resources – gold and diamonds and bauxiteand rainforest timber and shrimp fisheries. That is, the incoming foreign investor meets with the relevant minister(s), offers incentives/rewards, and is allowed or encouraged to write his/her own investment agreement, the terms of which remain unpublished. The sole exception to date was the rainforest logging and milling agreement for 25 years with the Malaysian company SamLing/Barama in 1991, written in Malaysian English, which was leaked in 1996 (Colchester 1997; Sizer 1996). For the ministers in 2016, XOM was just another carpetbagger, and the tens or hundreds of billions of dollars' worth of petroleum were conceptually no different from the millions of dollars' worth of timber.

Notes

[1] I use 'XOM' to represent the consortium of Esso Exploration and Production Guyana Ltd. (EEPGL), Hess Guyana Exploration Ltd. of the USA, and China National Offshore Oil Corporation (CNOOC), Nexen Petroleum Guyana Ltd., the Stabroek tract operator (EEPGL itself), and EEPGL's parent company, ExxonMobil Global Group, because it is oftenunclear in the available documents which entity is legally responsible for what still-in-draft Local Content Policy will be implemented mostly by Guyanese selling or renting land to the oil men (Kaieteur News 2021b).

[2] The companies that have blocks in the deep water area, offshore Guyana, are: Repsol and Tullow Oil (the Kanuku Block); Tullow (the Orinduik Block); Anadarko (the Roraima Block); Ratio Oil (the Kaieteur Block); ExxonMobil, CNOOC Nexen and Hess (the Stabroek Block); ExxonMobil, Mid-Atlantic and JHI (the Canje Block); CGX (the Demeraraand Corentyne blocks); ON Energy; and Nabi. All were granted contracts during the PPP/C's time in office (Stabroek News 2019). Note that although 'block' is commonly used in the press in Guyana to refer to an individual government-awarded petroleum concession, 'block' is defined in PEPA (see below) as a geographic rectangle covering 8,550 ha. The correct term for the above-mentioned blocks is 'tract'

[3] https://www.oggn.website/2021/11/12/audio-rough-transcript-of-yellowtail-exxon-epa-meeting-on-nov-11th-2021/

[4] https://www.gra.gov.gy/other-major-services/customs-petroleum-unit/

[5] https://op.gov.gy/index.php/2018/08/20/ministry-of-the-presidency-department-of-energy-terms-of-reference-for-office-manager/

6. https://parliament.gov.gy/about-parliament/parliamentarian/bharrat-jagdeo

References

Marcus Colchester (1997) Guyana, Fragile Frontier: Loggers, Miners and Forest Peoples, Ian Randle Publishers.

Steve Coll (2012) Private Empire: ExxonMobil and American Power, The Penguin Press.

Sanjeev Datadin (2020) The need for parliamentary oversight, *Oil Dorado*?,London: Bite-Sized Books pp 51-54, second edition.

Department of Public Information (2019) Press release – Restructuring ofGFC, GGMC, 7 November. https://nre.gov.gy/2019/11/07/press-release- restructuring-of-gfc-ggmc/

Thomas W Donovan (2004) Challenges to the territorial integrity of Guyana: Alegal analysis, Georgia Journal of International & Comparative Law, Vol.32 pp 661-724

Dominic Gaskin (2018) Response to some of the comments about my presentation at oil and gas seminar, Stabroek News, 14 March. https://www.stabroeknews.com/2018/opinion/letters/03/14/response-to- some-of-the-comments-about-my-presentation-at-oil-and-gas-seminar/

Government Information News Agency (2017) Guyana's Sovereign Wealth Fund for public consultation, 29 March. https://dpi.gov.gy/guyanas-sovereign-wealth-fund-for-public-consultation/

Guyana Times (2021) Audit of pre-contract costs must be a priority – Ram,18 January. https://guyanatimesgy.com/audit-of-pre-contract-costs-must- be-a-priority-ram/

iNews Guyana (2019) British firm paid US$300,000 to audit US$460m.Exxon pre-contract costs, 17 December.

https://www.inewsguyana.com/british-firm-paid-us300000-to-audit- us460m-exxon-pre-contract-costs/

Kaieteur News (2021a) Clyde and Co. report is enough to push for renegotiation – Ram, 22 January. https://www.kaieteurnewsonline.com/2021/01/22/clyde-and-co-report-is-enough-to-push-for-renegotiation-ram/

Kaieteur News (2021b) We can't build FPSOs, so rent out your properties

2021VPJagdeo, April. https://www.kaieteurnewsonline.com/2021/04/15/we-cant-build-fpsos-so- rent-out-your-properties-vp-jagdeo/

Kaieteur News (2021c) Govt's. failure to meet 2-year audit deadline; Guyana is now forced to pay US$9.5B for Liza 1&2 Projects, November 4th. https://www.kaieteurnewsonline.com/2021/11/04/exxonmobil-will-now- recover-full-us9-5b-spending-on-liza-1-2-projects/

Kaieteur News (2021d) Jagdeo's excuse for Govt.'s failure to audit US$10B in Exxon's expenses 'misleading and unfortunate'– Chris Ram, 5 November

OilNOW (2017) Guyana-Suriname Basin ranked 2nd most prospective inthe world for oil, OilNOW. http://oilnow.gy/featured/guyana-suriname- basin-ranked-2nd-most-prospective-in-the-world-for-oil/

Abena Rockcliffe-Campbell (2018) US$18m ExxonMobil signing bonus…There is no paper trail of negotiations – Trotman tells Parliamentary Committee, Kaieteur News, 22 May. https://www.kaieteurnewsonline.com/2018/05/22/us18m-exxonmobil- signing-bonus-there-is-no-paper-trail-of-negotiations-trotman-tells- parliamentary-committee/

Nigel Sizer (1996) Profit Without Plunder: Reaping Revenue from Guyana'sTropical Forests without Destroying Them, World Resources Institute.

Stabroek News (2019) Companies say award of Canje oil block

licence was above board, 2 June.
https://www.stabroeknews.com/2019/news/guyana/06/02/com
panies-say- award-of-canje-oil-block-licence-was-above-
board/

Kiana Wilburg (2021) Jagdeo single-handedly dictates
Guyana's depletionpolicy to be 'drill baby drill!', Kaieteur
News, 3 January

About the contributor

Dr Janette Bulkan is an Associate Professor in the Department of Forest Resources Management in the Faculty of Forestry, University of British Columbia. She was Senior Social Scientist at the Iwokrama International Centre for Rainforest Conservation and Development from March 2000 to March 2003.

Chapter Fifteen

The Moray House Mensheviks

The Oil Bonanza in Guyana has resulted in much internal debate. John Mair finds a surprise: a bastion of free speech that seems to have become a one-sided platform

The Guyanese like a good argument, especially one lubricated with plenty of El Dorado (the drink). Rum shops are everywhere on street corners and in front rooms throughout the nation.

The big debate over the last decade has been about the oil boom; is it good or bad for the nation, what results will there be? The national forums for this debate are limited. The Parliament/National Assembly is too often the scene of cross-party hand-to-hand warfare that spills over into the courts. The national newspapers are firmly divided on political/racial lines on oil as on much else. The best-selling Kaieteur News is an outlier there: pro-Indo but firmly anti-oil day after day. That is down to the foibles of the owner Glenn Lall.

Creating a place for the national conversation

This is why David de Caires' creation The Stabroek News has such historical importance. It was set up in 1986 in the wake of the Forbes Burnham dictatorship and has faced many crosswinds since: paper rationing from Burnham's successors, boycotts by politicians, the then President Jagdeo withdrawing government advertising to try to cripple it. All failed.

De Caires was a one-off: an upper-class descendant of Portuguese indentured labourers, his family has done very well. Young David was sent to boarding school in the UK, naturally to Stonyhurst in Lancashire, a Roman Catholic Eton. Back home to Guyana a legal career beckoned. That did not satisfy him after a while so he became a journalist/editor by the back door. He simply set up a newspaper.

Over the years de Caires established the Stabroek News as the home of the national conversation. Its letters pages were the forum for open, and often long-winded debate, on all matters Guyanese. He believed in light-touch editing so that encouraged the prolix.

David was a firm believer in freedom of speech. I know first-hand as I wrote a daily column for him, when I was back in Guyana, under the nom de guerre Bill Cotton/Reform (a riff on Burnham's PNC Party which had rebranded as PNC/Reform to attempt to slough off the dictator's mantle).

Bill Cotton/Reform was pure scuttlebutt which day after day hit some big targets in amusing ways. It proved popular. David always published it, sometimes with a tinker or two. But he was very brave and the best editor with whom I have worked. His legacy lives on in the paper and the family residence Moray House in Camp Street Georgetown. That was donated by the family as a place for discussion after his death in 2008.

The Moray House Trust (MHT) has done some brilliant work preserving and highlighting Guyanese culture -- literature, theatre, art, and more. The Guyanese are very creative and very prolific. That part of the output would have pleased David who gave unstinting support to local artists of all shades in person and in the paper.

Oiling the arguments?

The MHT should also be the place for informed discussion on Oil Dorado. To quote their founding statement 'a culture thrives and develops where ideas circulate and are robustly debated and interrogated'.

In recent years, though, their sights have become rather blinkered and one-sided. Not free speech so much as 'let's bash the government and the oil companies' speech. David might not recognise this Moray Trust as his progeny even though it is headed by his daughter Isabelle who lives mostly in the UK.

It is in the public sphere of their discussions on oil with which I take most issue. Not to put too fine a point on it, they are very one-sided.

How many sides to a debate?

I have analysed the last five years of Moray House oil discussions, both in-person and virtually online during the pandemic. As far as I could find they were sixteen events with titles ranging from the general 'What will oil do for Guyana?' to the inquisitive 'Guyana's oil - road to perdition or prosperity?' to the provocative 'Will oil and gas fuel conflict in Guyana?' (which is Guyanese-speak for black/brown racial conflict).

The titles speak for themselves but more important is the casting of those discussions. Looking as hard as I can, I only found one openly pro-PPP (the current government) speaker, Charles Ransom Jr. He is a British-trained lawyer; now he's a government minister. There are a few neutrals like Greg Quinn, the then British High Commissioner, Srdan Deric of the UN, and David Jessop then of the Caribbean Council, but the large majority of MHT speakers are government critics of one sort or another, some representing NGOs, some not.

The 'usual suspects'

The central cast or 'usual suspects' is quite small. Christopher Ram, brilliant accountant turned lawyer. He has devoted the last decade to becoming an oil and oil contract expert. His series in the Stabroek News on 'What every man, woman and child in British Guiana should know about oil' is masterly. Vincent Adams was the head of the Environment Protection Agency in the previous regime. It is said he wanted to be the oil minister but his party were the minority of the APNU Coalition. Jan Mangal, Guyanese, but who, as many others, emigrated to the USA, was adviser on oil to the previous President David Granger who disposed of his services. Melinda Janki, a lawyer with experience in both the UK and Guyana, some in oil. Since her return 'home' in 1994 she has been a thorn in the side of all governments in Guyana and further afield. Tarron Khemraj, an émigré professor of economics in the USA. Annette Ajoon, an environmentalist, a product of one of the great Indo-Guyanese families. Professor Clive Thomas, a respected economist who became the (muted) tsar of anti-corruption in the previous regime. Plus representatives from NGOs (non-government organisations) like TIGI (Transparency Institute Guyana Inc), the Amerindian People's Association, the Guyana National Youth Council, and the feminist group Red Thread. Many of these 'usual suspects' have cruised around in each other's company for decades in various micro parties.

But, as too often is the case in Guyana, it is never clear how many troops these NGOs have and whom they represent. There is always the suspicion that they are letterhead bodies: middle class and able to generate plenty of noise but based on small foundations.

Many of the Moray House oil/gas panellists do have specialist knowledge but, alas, they often bring an agenda. That varies from 'leave the oil in the ground' to 'watch out for oil spills' to 'what will the native people -- Amerindians -- get from oil?' to corrupt politicians led astray by Big Oil and damage to turtles. If there are sores to be picked in the case for Oil Dorado, they will pick them

Very few of the central cast can be said to have clean hands and open minds when it comes to Guyana oil and gas. That is the tragedy. They differ in degree but in general they are against. David de Caires might agree with some of their positions. Hegel was right: Nothing wrong with good arguments if they come to sensible agreed conclusions which benefit the nation. But these debates do seem to me to rather one-sided.

Oil Dorado is here. Guyana is the big, maybe the biggest, current oil 'play' in South America, the Caribbean, and the World. The sensible debates to be had are about local content and local control, the benefits to all the nation and life after oil.

Is it not too late for the Moray House Mensheviks to extend their horizons to the real debates? David de Caires would approve. History is not on their side. Nor the nation?

About the contributor

John Mair was born in British Guiana. He returns often and sometimes attends Moray House debates whilst there.

Chapter Sixteen

Is it Guyana's time? (2022)

GHK Lall is the most articulate of newspaper columnists in Guyana. With his Guyanese heritage and his background in First World finance in Wall Street he is in a unique position to assess the hopes and fears for his native land

Guyana is on the express track to the potential of greatness that has always somehow ended up outside of its reaching, tentative grasp. Now it must clutch more firmly to its fabled promise and get a real taste of what its essences could mean. The arrival of oil in torrential quantities and of a higher quality has changed the domestic dynamics of this poor nation. With the arrival of billions of barrels of this black gold literally gushing like geysers from below its seabed, there is the opening for so much more to capitalize on the mushroom of downstream and ancillary avenues to make money, and for this Guyana to be more than a dot on the map.

The time is now for this most talked-about nation across the globe to assume its mantle as the place to be, the society on a shining sea, with so much of its promise brightly beckoning, for those who come to sow and reap what could be a bountiful harvest from this Oil Dorado and its fossil fuel bonanza.

Why invest in Oil Dorado?

Everybody who is anybody, and those aspiring to be somebody, is looking to put down an investment stake in Guyana, to take advantage of the moment, and to amplify their own prospects. Nobody wants to be left behind, to slap themselves with 'what if' and letting Guyana go by unexplored. Guyana is the stuff of dreams; legends long spoken around local campfires in hushed tones, the native lore that makes the eyes light up with awe of what could be.

Well, they are all rising to the fore, coming to past, and in the lifetime of this present generation of Guyanese, and they must all work diligently to get matters right, on an even keel, for the full speed ahead acceleration that the times call in this its spellbinding Age of Oil.

From princes to professionals to peasants to paupers and all in between, the mentality has to be of all hands tight on the deck, all shoulders to the wheel, so that the world at its feet doesn't trip them all up. There is such a thing as going too fast, and so there must be care, so that there is ongoing calibration and continuing adjustment, the necessary amendments. Out of sheer necessity, there has to be the right people to manage this overwhelming wealth that can discombobulate even the wisest, the most seasoned in this field, and with these confluences all rushing forward and rising simultaneously.

Why not invest in Oil Dorado?

Guyana, this new Oil Dorado to an intrigued and mesmerized investment world, offers so much to so many, and so swiftly. It already is deemed, and not without accuracy as the fabled El Dorado, and long after Sir Walter Raleigh came probing with visions of glory dancing in his head. Guyana, as it stands today, has all going for it to become this new, unmatched metropolis, 'Arabia on the Demerara' and an Atlantis that overcomes its inhibitions and limitations, and endures. But it must be said again and again that it must get its internal dynamics, and its environmental ambience, in smoother order, and to just that right, stabilizing fashion, and to the comforting degree, that it lures those knocking on its door. Their work and vision have to be a combination of expansive intellect, rare insight, and on- the-run inspiration.

Guyana cannot be the Guyana of old, the one that is always grappling to fathom itself, to appreciate its bounties. The Guyanese people need to grow, and they must. Their long, enfeebling underbelly must be paid attention to, addressed with alacrity and energy. It is of politics, the passions that dominate and derail, and which could make them into their own worst enemies in this their brilliant season in the sun. There must be the readiness to search for, find, and develop the national character that is found appealing by those coming to their shores to do better for themselves, and for the Guyanese people. They must overcome their demons, banish their fears and nightmares, some imagined, some all too real. They have guests already in country, and there are many more on the way.

The best in a hospitable nature ought to be on display at all times, so that the very best can come their way, into their hands. It calls for a lot from them, and they must manifest the courage and the class, and the character also, to rise to the occasion. Only with this kind of outlook on their gifts will they put themselves in a position to reap the sweets of their riches, be such from oil or the hosts of other offshoots generated by its discoveries, which still continue at thrilling speeds.

Guyana Mean Time?

The Guyanese people must be of that singular mind that envisions the best from this oil, and this is despite a weak and shaky start. There is a world of work to do, endless areas to cover, and they all must learn to adapt as their world changes at breakneck speed. Their language must be new, their instincts better; but the learning curve is long, and can be steep, if not approached sensibly. Already yesterday's development is ancient history, with newer urgencies and vibrancies leading the charge in this the newest, most attractive oil frontier on the planet. In view of all that is taking place on the ground, and the swarms of almost overnight sensations, the most alluring oil frontier in the world may be better stated as the most desirable frontier for anything. Period.

This is 'Guyana time', and its people can have the time of their lives. There is no limit to what can be, but it comes at a price. Discipline. Vision. Duty. Self-respect. Self-sacrifice. Leaders must truly lead, and this flows from governing expansively and sagaciously. People must participate in the fullness of their abilities, and in the availability of opportunities for them to experience the tingling sensations of what is tangible -- all of the many tendrils of that - with this oil. Doors must be open wide to welcome those who come laden with ideas and investment interests, so that the street of reward is two-way. It could be, it just has to be, for there is no other, or else it is better that the oil is not there. The reality is that it is there, and it is ripe and ready.

Beyond Walter Raleigh's wildest dreams

The numbers are unbelievable, and this is regardless of what is the measuring rod employed. Oil is in the billions of barrels, a heap of it highly likely still unaccounted for, waiting for the seismic touch, the sharp prick of the drill to uncover its charms. Returns on capital have already proven to be astronomical, be the tool of calculus employed plain old percentages, or as reckoned in the bullion of good old banknotes. And these are representative of the beginning only. Democracy is in its cradle, but with the right touches, the vitally necessary embracing and warming actions, Guyana's way of life can, with concerted effort and the smooth passage of time, take its rightful place among the free, inclusive, tolerant, and well-regarded nations of the world.

There is so much at stake in Guyana, so much going on, so much that is irresistible, from suites to house, compounds to house compounds of a different nature, plants to be staffed and equipped and wired, expert services to provide, and very direly needed, and many other vacuums and broad spaces to occupy with delightful results. They are all there for the taking, for the coming and experiencing, and for the sharing in what has to be, can only be, the newest wonder of the world.

This is the Guyana story, as it stands today on the cusp of sprawling, flourishing, prosperity, once managed correctly and prudently. The evolution of Guyana through its oil wealth is nothing less than a revolution; may it be a golden one. It is a beautiful story, one that has all the elements to be among the great ones told.

About the contributor

GHK Lall was born in Guyana but lived for over thirty years in the US, twenty of them working in Wall Street. He is a former Securities and Investment Principal. Since returning to Guyana, he has chaired the Guyana Gold Board, written a regular column in a local newspaper and volunteered as a teacher and in a hospice.

Chapter Seventeen

A new age dawns, finally (2019)

In a piece written in 2019 Christopher Ram argues that the clues were always there but it has taken decades of hope – and border disputes – for oil to be finally realised

A quest that began in earnest some 170 years ago will soon become reality as Guyana – often the forgotten former British colony in South America – is set to become a top oil and gas producer on a per-capita basis in just one year. Between May 2015 and January 2019, ExxonMobil, the American oil giant, announced 12 'high-impact discoveries of oil and gas' with estimated gross recoverable resource of between four and five billion oil-equivalent barrels. (In 2020 that figure was up to 8bn.)

In 1929, there was a banner headline in one of the colony's newspapers which screamed 'Every Man, Woman and Child Must Become Oil- Minded!' Long before that, indications of Guyana's offshore oil capabilities came from reports of the early Dutch explorers who noted the occurrence of flotsam pitch, while in 1917 a person described in all the records only as J. Harrison discovered a thin deposit of heavy oil (pitch) near Krunkenae Point, on the west coast of the Waini River, in Region 1.[1] Following those earlier surface oil indications, the first hole was drilled at a site northwest of the Waini Mouth at the top of Guyana.

While a few drops of heavy oil were observed, the thickness of sediments was found inadequate for the formation of oil. Later wells drilled for water encountered seepages of gas, the most significant of which took place at Bath Estate on the bank of the Berbice River, which for many years was used for cooking purposes.

In 1939, 11 years after British Guiana had become a Crown colony,[2] its new legislative council passed the Petroleum Production Act providing for the vesting in the Crown the property in petroleum and natural gas and making provision for the issue of separate licences for prospecting and exploration.One year earlier, Trinidad Leaseholds Co. Ltd had been granted the first oilprospecting licence but abandoned it in 1942.[3]

In 1958, a one-month offshore marine reconnaissance seismic survey was carried out by subsidiaries of Standard Oil of California, and this was followed by several aeromagnetic surveys conducted between 1956 and 1965 traversing the onshore Takutu Basin.[4] Intrigued by the 1965 survey, Phoenix Oil Co of Canada showed interest in the Takutu Basin, and was granted acreage in 1966, but which it never took up.[5]

Decades of hope

In the five decades from the 1960s and up to the first decade of the 21st century, at least 20 companies principally from the USA, Canada and France, of which the most prominent were Shell Conoco/Tenneco, Home Oil and Mobil, made trial investigations.

Additionally, there wereorganisations like the UNDP, World Bank and CIDA, which financedvarious studies in the search for oil. The most encouraging phase of activityin Guyana was clearly in the Takutu Basin located in the south-western partof the country.

A significant activity to note within that time period is Home Oil of Canada,which drilled two wells in 1981 and 1982, of which the second well, Karanambo-1, produced 400 barrels of oil per day, apparently from fractured Apoteri Volcanics.[6]

Despite this result, Home Oil eventually abandoned thewell due to failure in acquiring additional partners to finance further drilling.

In the last ten years of the last century, a few other oil companies had sought and subsequently obtained prospecting and exploration licences in Guyana. At present, Nabi Oil and Gas, ON Energy, Tullow, Repsol, CGX Resources, Eco Atlantic Oil and Gas, Mid Atlantic Guyana, Esso and JHI Associates, CNOOC Nexen and Hess, Anadarko, Ratio Energy/Ratio Guyana and, of course, ExxonMobil, all have licences or are in partnership with a licence holder to prospect and explore.

Licence holders with estimated hectares (2019)

Location	Block	Estimated Hectares	Licensee	Joint Venture Partner
Inland	Takutu Basin	1,000,000	Nil	Nil
Coastal	Mahaicony	260,000	Nabi Oil &Gas Inc.	Nil
	Berbice	333,000	ON Energy	Nil
Shelf	Kanuku	660,000	Repsol	Tullow
	Corentyne	630,000	CGX Resources Inc.	Nil
	Orinduik	180,000	Tullow	Eco Atlantic Oil and Gas
Deep-water	Canje	611,000	Mid Atlantic Guyana Inc.	Esso & JHI Associates
	Stabroek	2,700,000	Esso	CNOOC Nexen and Hess
Ultra-deep-water	Roraima	1,990,000	Anadarko	Nil
	Kaieteur	1,360,000	Ratio Energy Inc /Ratio Guyana Inc	Esso

Location of the offshore petroleum blocks

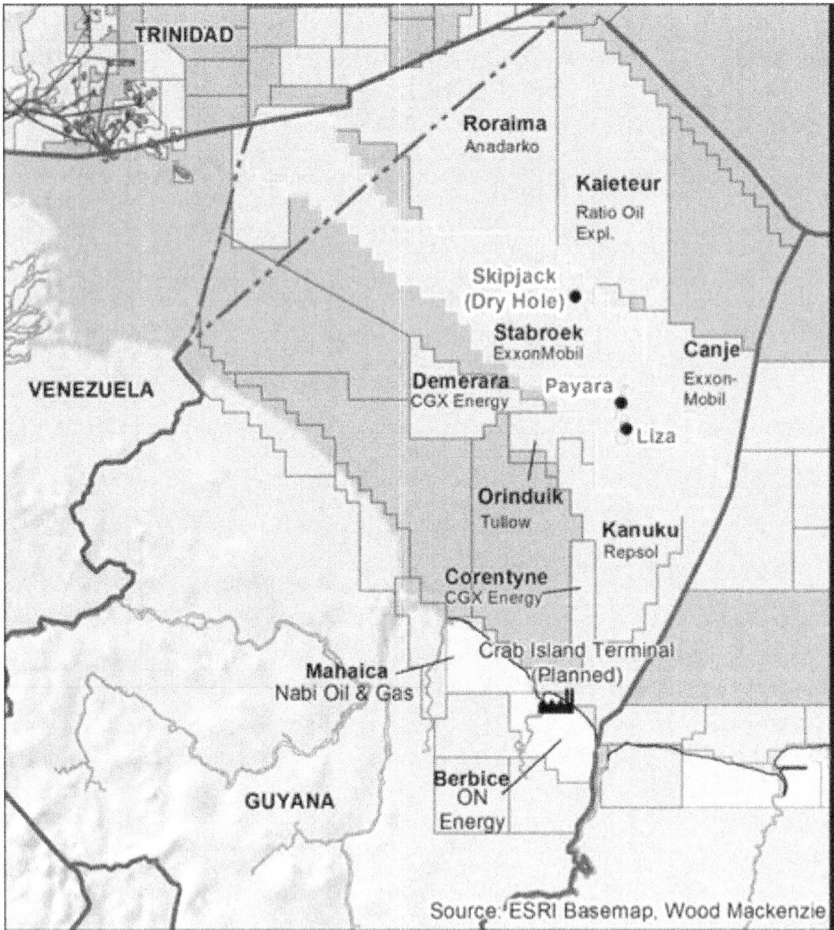

TRINIDAD

Roraima
Anadarko

Kaieteur
Ratio Oil
Expl.

Skipjack
(Dry Hole)

Stabroek
ExxonMobil

Canje
Exxon-
Mobil

Demerara
CGX Energy

Payara

Liza

VENEZUELA

Orinduik
Tullow

Kanuku
Repsol

Corentyne
CGX Energy

Crab Island Terminal
(Planned)

Mahaica
Nabi Oil & Gas

Berbice
ON
Energy

GUYANA

Source: ESRI Basemap, Wood Mackenzie

However, in its quest for oil, Guyana was hampered by the strong-arm tactics of two of its neighbours – Suriname and Venezuela.

Guyana-Venezuela border controversy

Guyana's and Venezuela's strained relations have their origin in the colonisation of the Americas by competing European powers during an era when boundaries were not properly defined. A more formal approach to border-setting began in 1841 when Venezuela submitted to Great Britain a formal proposal for a boundary between it and the then-British Guiana.

Britain showed little urgency in addressing the matter even after receiving a 10,000-word dispatch[7] from Richard Olney, then secretary of state of the United States, demanding from the British a decision on whether it would submit the question to impartial arbitration. The response was dismissive and caused President Cleveland to be 'mad clean through' when he read the reply.

Good sense later prevailed and, in 1897, an arbitral tribunal was establishedto determine the boundary between the two countries. It was agreed amongthe parties that the result of the proceeds of the tribunal of arbitration would constitute a full, perfect and final settlement of all the questions referred to the arbitrators.

The decision of the tribunal of 1899 was unanimous and was given effect toby a joint Venezuelan/British Mixed Boundary Commission in a demarcation exercise in 1901-1905. Thereafter, the story became wrapped up in international intrigue, accusations of bribery and alleged collusion bythe British and American governments to keep out a left-leaning government in British Guiana, before independence from Britain. That led to what is referred to as the Geneva Agreement of 1966 agreed between the UK and Venezuela to resolve the controversy over the frontier between Venezuela and British Guiana.

Despite the agreement, Venezuela has remained steadfast in its claim, posinga great threat to Guyana's sovereignty and by extension its oil prospects. Following the announcement of the early discoveries, the energy and petroleum commission of the national assembly in Venezuela rejected the oil operations in the Essequibo region,[8] claiming that it violated the Genevaagreement of 1966 and Article 10 its constitution.[9] In fact, in 2015 the President of Venezuela issued a decree claiming the maritime area in whichthe oil exploration was being done, which he subsequently recalled.[10]

Legally, the fate of the controversy now rests with the International Court ofJustice to which the matter has been taken by Guyana following the failure of a United Nations process, which saw the appointment of a good officer to resolve the controversy. Venezuela has refused to participate in the process.Practically, Guyana, it seems,

is relying on the presence of a major Americanoil company in the controverted maritime territory to help protect its rights.

Guyana-Suriname border dispute

The border dispute between Guyana and Suriname had its genesis in the 18th century, when colonial powers (Great Britain and Netherlands) fought overland. In 1967, the government of Suriname stated that, in a treaty signed in 1799 between the Dutch and the British, all of the territory west of the Corentyne River was ceded to the colony of Berbice and the border was the left bank of the Corentyne from its mouth to its source. The Suriname government claimed that the Corentyne is a national river lying within its territory and not a boundary river.

Guyana's position was that the south-eastern boundary between Guyana andSuriname was determined by international agreement among the governments of Brazil, Great Britain and the Netherlands in 1936.

The concrete evidence of that agreement is the tri-junction point at the headof the Kutari River where their three territories touched. It took more than 150 years for a definitive resolution to permanently settle the correct boundary between Berbice and Suriname. This was achieved in 2007 after Guyana had initiated proceedings for a judicial settlement under the United Nations Convention on the Law of the Sea, to which both countries were signatories.

Notes

[1] United Nations Technical Assistance Board, Reporting on the Prospecting for oil in British Guiana, United Nations: New York, 1965 pp 8-9
[2] Mohamed Shahabudeen (1978) Constitutional Development in Guyana 1621-1978,Georgetown: Guyana Printers Ltd.
[3] Exploration Consultants Ltd, Guyana Petroleum Exploration

Appraisal,Guyana Basin, Vol. 1, 1985 pp 7-13

[4] UNDP reports 1965 and 1966

[5] Exploration Consultants Ltd, Guyana Petroleum Exploration Appraisal,Guyana Basin, Vol. 1, 1985 pp 7-13

[6] ibid

[7] A dispatch made famous for the original articulation of the Monroe Doctrine in a written communication to a foreign government. See Cedric L.Joseph, Anglo-American Diplomacy and the Reopening of the Guyana- Venezuela Border Controversy, 1961-1966, Trafford Publishing p. 50

[8] Denis Chabrol, Venezuela says oil operations in Guyana violates agreement, Demerara Waves, Georgetown, 17 March 2017. http://demerarawaves.com/2017/03/17/venezuela-says-oil-operations-in- guyana-violates agreement/

[9] The Bolivarian Constitution of Venezuela, article 10

[10] Denis Chabrol op cit

About the contributor

Christopher Ram is an attorney-at-law and chartered accountant with active practices in both fields. This chapter is an adaptation of a project paper submitted by the author under a 2017/18 full-time distance learning programme for a Master of Law in Oil and Gas Law at Reading University in the UK. It was awarded a distinction.

Chapter Eighteen

Why I've invested in Oil Dorado

Investors in emerging markets need to be patient and to accept some volatility on their journey. But with a little diversification and a keen eye on governance they can then expect higher returns. Nowhere on the planet is this now more keenly observable than in Guyana, advises Neil Passmore

My colleagues and I have been visiting and investing in the country for over six years. I have made over 25 trips to the country so far and have more capital deployed there than any independent financial adviser would likely recommend. I have advised a variety of Guyanese clients and helped introduce many investors to the country.

I have lost as well as made money, had the occasional dispute and plenty of disappointments. But I continue to increase my exposure. Here is why I am so positive, and what I have learned so far.

Look on the bright side

Political access is excellent, friendly and co-operative: if you want to engage with a government official you can usually get to them quickly. The rule of law is very strong. The system is mainly based on English common law, the judiciary is sizeable, of decent quality and independent. A number of good law firms exist. A literate workforce awaits you. Education standards are high – you face smart, literate and usually worldly people. You can hire well and get things done. Corruption is relatively low – there is a degree of political patronage, but there is not a 'facilitation fee' culture. Most importantly, English is the first language which makes life simple in many, many ways.

Opportunity knocks all the time

The scale is vast. Guyana's Gross Domestic Product (GDP) is set to triple in the next five years. Some of the very obvious asset classes have started to rally. Exploration acreage, real estate, and the local stock market have broken out in valuation, but even there, attractively priced assets still exist when viewed on a global basis. More broadly, many other brilliant opportunities are still almost unexplored.

Investment success hinges principally on execution and oversight, not on opportunity spotting. Almost any idea from equipment rental to coffee shops will be a good one. But good execution, competent management at all levels, strong governance, and ensuring returns flow to shareholders rather than leaking to other stakeholders is key to securing the return on capital that should be attainable. Guyana is now on the path to becoming one of the world's richest countries per capita.

Pitfalls and pratfalls

The country has a huge face-to-face culture in business. Email is not always reliably used. A great deal of business is done in person. It bears saying but watch out for pirates and pick your partners carefully. The best deal you can find is unlikely to be the first one you bump into off the plane. Take your time. Be patient. Guyana can be bureaucratic. Its processes work and so do the checks and balances, but they can take time. The response to newcomers trying to upturn the system on their first trip to the bank or stock exchange is as welcome by the heads of those institutions in Guyana as it would be anywhere in the world!

The Guyanese can be overly pessimistic: stand by for some grumbling, but don't be deterred. I have so far only convinced a few that the perceived Guyana-centric woes are in fact no better in the UK.

Collaboration is not yet a widely held or cherished concept. Business in many sectors in Guyana has been a zero-sum game for a long time. If I sell you a car it will in part be because you don't buy one from my rival; the mentality of peer companies collectively growing end markets is not familiar, albeit economic growth is changing this.

Brickbats and bouquets

I have acted as an adviser raising money for oil explorers and operating companies in Guyana. I have invested in the stock market and real estate. I have founded an agriculture company. I have brilliant business partners in country, but like all relationships a huge amount of time must continually be invested in them. My colleagues and I try to be in the country every quarter, and preferably every month.

I worry physical security may worsen, albeit the government is working hard to ensure this does not become the case. Personally, I have had no first-hand bad experiences and have taken my family to Guyana for holidays.

Everything works better when I steer and empower my local Guyanese team and partners rather than trying to visibly do it myself. The same is true of taking advice from the right advisers and supporters locally; but I need to be present.

I wish I had put more capital into passive investments with good listed operating companies there. Local investors evaluate their listee businesses in very old fashioned and sensible ways, focusing on balance sheet strength and cash flows. The Guyanese, like many who have had it fairly tough for a while, are excellent business operators. In Guyana, use the High Commissioners and investment agencies/authorities that are there as they are excellent. So too are the heads of the main banks, who are insightful on where the market is moving.

Keep a low profile but contribute to the community. If you have found political support slow at points, still let the government take some credit for your achievements anyway.

All said, remind yourself frequently of the universal truths I started this piece with; investors in emerging markets need to be patient and accept some volatility on their journey. We are seeing one such window at the moment.

And finally, drink as much coconut water as you can. It keeps you hydrated by day, mixes well with rum by night, and you'll be lifting my sales!

About the contributor

Neil Passmore is a former military helicopter pilot. He is a very active investor in Oil Dorado.

SECTION THREE: A LITTLE LIGHT HISTORY . . . OR AT LEAST 2019

John Mair

This section is a deliberate look back to the heady early days of 2019 and the hopes of that year. We feature four prominent decision-makers of the time (or now) from the then prime minister to the current chief adviser on petroleum.

First off, the Hon. Moses Nagamootoo, then PM and minister of information. He had wanted to be PPP president but left the party when passed over. Instead, he crossed the floor. In 2019, he was optimistic: 'With the significant amount of money expected to flow to Guyana, the government has begun serious planning on how to utilise the expected oil resources to benefit all our people.'

The people voted him and his government out of office in March 2020. It took five months for them to stop trying to dispute the result. The new government took over after a period of attempted election rigging stopped by international pressure. Nagamootoo is now in (permanent?) exile in Liliendaal, East Coast Demerara.

Robert Persaud is the nearly man who has come again. He is former ministerof natural resources in Guyana. He lost office in March 2015 just in time to award an oil franchise to some close colleagues. Exxon announced its first discovery in May 2015. Robert would also have liked to have been the PPP president. That was not to be. Instead, he came back from a 'sabbatical' in the US to resume office, this time as foreign secretary, when his party (finally) won the 2020 election. Penned in 2019, in 'Is Guyana ready for prime time?', he looks forward to the future rather than dwelling on the past.'Oil will be ours to determine whether it will be a curse or cure,' he says, 'and I'm confident it will be one of the many cures to our decades-old social and economic setbacks. The work of attaining the elusive goal of national prosperity has now started with the beckoning of oil and gas!'

In 2019 Bobby Gossai was a Guyanese studying for a PhD at, inevitably, the University of Aberdeen (most of the oil experts in Guyana have been there). In 2023 he is the government's chief adviser on petroleum. In 'A blueprint for sustained success', he argues that a disciplined stewardship of the windfall from Guyana's new oil and gas finds could leadto great long-term prosperity. That means macro-economic action. Now. He concludes: 'One major imperative for Guyana is to focus on removing barriers to productivity across five key areas of the economy: the resources sector itself; resource rider sectors such as utilities and construction; manufacturing; local services such as retail trade and financial services; and agriculture.'

Lessons from the heady early days - four years ago - of oil in Guyana.

Chapter Nineteen

Foreword to Oil Dorado? first edition, 2019

Moses V. Nagamootoo, prime minister and minister of public information (2015 - 2020)

As this hitherto unknown country, renamed the Co-operative Republic of Guyana from its colonial appellation 'British Guiana', approaches its Golden Jubilee as a Republic in 2020, its new image as the promising major oil producer is that of the fabled El Dorado – the lost city of gold.

With a population of less than one million people, mostly descendants of African slaves and Indian indentured labourers who were once tied to the British colonial sugar plantocracy, Guyana is today a hot point for industry projections and opinions.

Its numerous, huge offshore oil finds started in 2015. The ExxonMobil-led consortium – Exxon, HESS and CNOOC Petroleum – has announced 'First Oil' in the coming months. With two huge new discoveries, the number of wells has increased to 12 in only one area – the Stabroek Block, which is some 120km within Guyana's EEZ.

Exxon has said that there is potential for at least five floating production storage and offloading vessels that can produce more than 750,000 barrels of oil per day by 2025! That has influenced one American writer, Steve LeVine, in an article titled, 'The surprising next oil superpower', to describe Guyana as being 'on the cusp of becoming one of the world's wealthiest nations'. LeVine projected that at US$60 a barrel, Guyana could receive more than US$5bn a year in revenue.

The Norwegian consultant, Rystad Energy, estimated that Guyana stood to earn more than $6bn in royalties and taxes annually by the end of 2020. With the significant amount of money expected to flow to Guyana, the government has begun serious planning on how to utilise the expected oil resources to benefit all our people. The government has crafted a solid legalframework to protect our oil and gas wealth under a Natural Resources FundAct – Guyana's version of a sovereign wealth fund.

Further, investment in infrastructures and spending on social services, including education, health and housing, will be guided by rigid fiscal rulesas well as the Guyana Green State Development Strategy (GSDS). Meanwhile, the Guyana National Upstream Oil and Gas Policy and a LocalContent Policy have been finalised.

To update and develop its policies, regulations and legislation, Guyana has received support from several countries and organisations: the United Nations Development Programme (UNDP), the World Bank, United States, Kingdom of Norway, Trinidad and Tobago, World Wildlife Fund, European Union, Canada, Chile, Mexico, the Russian Federation, and Conservation International (CI).

Effective management of the oil and gas sector is crucial to its success. Towards this aim, an energy department has been established under the auspices of the ministry of the presidency, while a petroleum department hasbeen added to the ministry of natural resources. Upon the passage of a Petroleum Commission Bill, a broad-based commission will be established to regulate the oil and gas sector to ensure that the interests of the people ofGuyana are protected.

About the contributor

Moses Nagamootoo was prime minister of Guyana from 2015-2020. He is a veteran politician who 'crossed the floor' from the PPP to the newly-formed AFC (Alliance for Change) when his presidential ambitions were thwarted. He and his coalition partners lost the next election in March 2020 but did not resign until August 2020. He is now retired – hurt?

Chapter Twenty

Is Guyana ready for oil prime time?

The first oil came in December 2019 (or before). In the next five years Guyana will become one of largest oil producers in the world. Here, former oil minister, now Foreign Secretary, Robert Persaud looked both backwards and forwards from 2019

The initial – and long – history of looking for oil in Guyana

One of the riskiest of all businesses is oil and gas (O&G) exploration. The gamble climbs exponentially if it is taking place in a virgin basin which not yet proven its commercial potential. O&G projects are by nature also risky venturesdue to their complex nature, potentially environmental impact, and high operational costs. This risk balloons for O&G exploration ventures in new frontiers. And then came Guyana.

Guyana's offshore, up until early 2015, was considered not only high-risk but also both unexplored and underexplored. But that was all to change.

First to be looked at was the Eagle 1 well, a 100 per cent undertaking by the Canadian business CGX which had received its petroleum agreement (PA) and petroleum prospecting licence (PPL). This well was estimated at 60 days of drilling, but due to weather and mechanical delays the drilling period hadto be extended by another 30 days. The original budget was $55m but it went over by about $22m (all figures in US dollars). The well encounteredoil but not in a commercial quantity.

Second was the Jaguar 1 well – a consortium of Repsol, YPF Guyana, CGX, and Tullow, which having received its PPL, launched the well-drilling. This was to be the deepest well drilled in the Guyana-Suriname Basin at a projected depth of 6,500 metres over 180 days. Drilling started in February 2012 and by early July 2012, having reached 4,876 metres, operations had to be abandoned. The well was plugged without reaching its primary objective. Then, in 2013, things became even riskier for oil exploration companies operating in the Guyanese offshore as Venezuela's thirst for hydrocarbon grew. In October, the Venezuelan navy seized, in Guyana's territorial water,the Teknik Perdana, an oil exploration ship contracted by the US company, Anadarko.

The determination of Esso Exploration and Production Guyana Limited (EEPGL), the local affiliate of ExxonMobil, must be commended in going forward with its planned exploration campaign. Faced not only with the existing risks but also the declining global oil price, the company pressed onleading to the May 2015 'world-class discovery' at Liza 1 in the Stabroek Block.

The exploration company's subsequent discoveries did not come at a small price tag. The 12 discoveries by ExxonMobil amount to in excess of six billion barrels of oil and yet to be officially confirmed stupendous amount of gas to power the country; they make Guyana a regional industrial hub andeven an exporter.

Playing catch-up

Are we ready for oil prime time? Or more specifically, are we ready for an economy where the oil and gas sector can be the tallest pillar? And to answer the obvious question – what did we do to prepare for commercial oil production in Guyana?

With limited resources there was only so much realistically that could have been done ahead of a commercial discovery curve. However, not lacking was the political will and national enthusiasm to get our nation in shape for this new, exciting bonanza sector.

And so, with all that we have now confirmed, and with all the loud buzz and much hype about when the first barrel of oil is pumped up and piped into a tanker for refining, we are racing against time. So, putting our house in full order cannot be deferred nor delayed.

Can Guyana turn its economy around?

For centuries, the productive pillars of the Guyana economy have been agriculture, fishing, mining and forestry. Then, in recent decades, we saw efforts at diversification with bold steps taken to develop the services sector with tourism and information and communication technology as the main areas of focus.

Now with oil production we ought to be culturally adaptive as a people for this additional new exciting economic endeavour and its expected interfacewith the traditional sectors.

But let us think deeply about this: the doubling of gross domestic product byone new sector (oil) can dwarf the impact of the other economic streams. Or even an astronomical growth in state revenue by this single new sector can create shockwaves for the other sectors both in terms of government's priority or even ordinary Guyanese interest in continued participation and investment by the private sector.

Oil revenue, according to an International Monetary Fund forecast, will initially be $350m per annum (and this is conservative as the spin-off benefits are not accounted for). Examples abound of how societies in all continents were improved, deformed and/or just simply transformed since commercial oil production began in 1840s in Pennsylvania, USA, and Baku, Azerbaijan, in 1871.

Gladly, we can all have faith the Guyanese people's ability to rise to the occasion. Our history has proven that we are versatile and resilient. Our cultural fabric, I am sure, will be able to adjust. Being aware and prepared, we must! Change should not be feared but rather be embraced with full knowledge of its impact.

It's Guyana's oil, not another's feast

With Guyana on the verge of being the next Caricom (Caribbean Economic Community) oil and gas giant, we see Trinidad and Tobago in overdrive mode to lecture and influence/infiltrate our course of developmentof this new sector, aided and abetted by some local players. Guyana, like a new beauty, is suddenly dazzling the eyes of our T&T counterparts andothers who are less bold.

There is, however, a feeling of entitlement by some in Trinidad and

Tobago vis-a-vis Guyana's oil and gas. A recent publication by Professor Anthony Bryan, of the University of the West Indies, reflected an emerging mindset that our O&G sector should be seen as a feast for Trinidad and Tobago (Bryan 2017).The article strikes a condescending tone, enumerates the perceived ills and problems of our society and, as we say, gives us 'a good bad mouthing' packaged as an analysis.

Our policymakers and private sector must be on guard. T&T is being very aggressive as it aims to get a chunk of the Guyanese O&G cake, potentially at the disadvantage of our own interests.

So, what should we do?

We must continue to encourage T&T., other Caricom states and countrieswith experience in O&G to invest and provide technical support, where necessary. This is not an excuse to dominate.

There must be a cap on employment of non-Guyanese when these skills are available, coupled with an aggressive multi-stakeholder programme on relevant skills development. The ongoing collaboration between the University of Guyana (UG) and the Ministry of Natural Resources/Department of Energy to train students has been encouraging.

The O&G companies must give preferential treatment or reserve services forqualified local suppliers, which are building experience and capacity for thisnew sector. T&T has 109 years of experience in oil and gas so its companies will, at this juncture, beat any local company on the requirementsfor experience and capacity.

A special incubation programme should be implemented for nascent local companies to build experience, expertise and capacity to adequately serve the sector.

Multinationals working in the O&G sector should be discouraged from working through their T&T affiliates and instead, directly pursue jointventures and collaboration with reputable Guyanese companies.

A special fund (revolving loans at concessionary rates) needs to be created to assist small and emerging businesses to support and work in the O&G sector.

We see, in other places, where the exclusion of nationals and local businesses in the O&G sector led to severe social and political repercussions.

Finalisation of a local content framework is needed to ensure meaningful participation of Guyanese and Guyanese businesses in the oil and gassectors.

A robust regulatory framework is also needed with modern and relevant legislation revision and additions, particularly the creation of the PetroleumCommission.

There should be stricter enforcement of all relevant regulations and laws concerning the oil and gas sector and holding oil companies accountable, including the promulgation of a depletion policy.

Let's not be naïve. Others are looking at our O&G sector for their next meal.We must demand our fair and just share. But, at the same time, we must be cognisant of the risks and work for the long-term viability of an O&G sectorthus enabling us for prime time as a serious player. It is Guyana's oil, not someone else's feast!

Conclusion

Opportunities and threats abound as this new sector emerges to augment other traditional and existing social and economic activities to reshape the economic landscape of Guyana. Let's be cognisant that the road ahead can be slippery. But a paradise is closer if we are able to summon the national courage and will to address our historic political ailments through constitutional reform, a refocus on shared prosperity and national unity, and greater respect from those afar who seek to dictate by either wilful economic influence or sheer disparagement of developing countries such as ours.

Oil will be ours to determine whether it will be a curse or cure. And I'm confident it will be one of the many cures to our decades-old social and economic setbacks. The work of attaining the elusive goal of nationalprosperity has now started with the beckoning of oil and gas!

Reference

Anthony Bryan (2017) https://theconversation.com/guyana-one-of-south- americas-poorest-countries-struck-oil-will-it-go-boom-or-bust-86108

About the contributor

Robert M. Persaud is the former cabinet minister of natural resources and the environment in Guyana. He was in office until May 2015. He became a consultant and a local content advocate whilst on 'sabbatical'. In 2020, he was appointed foreign secretary in the new PPP/C government.

Chapter Twenty-One

A blueprint for sustained success

A disciplined stewardship of the windfall from Guyana's new petroleum finds could lead to great long-term prosperity, said Bobby Gossai, Jr. in 2019. Today, he is the senior petroleum adviser to the government of Guyana. Will the ideas in his chapter bear fruit in policy?

A central issue for an oil management law is how to create practical and legal barriers that will inhibit subsequent governments from abandoning or evading the law while at the same time maintaining flexibility to meet changing conditions. Sovereignty means that any law passed by the current government is in principle subject to amendment or repeal by any future government. Still, measures can be taken even legislatively that may make it harder to change the law. For instance, in certain countries, it is possible to create special supermajority legislative approval and referenda requirements for changes in the law. Recent experience shows that referenda may be abused. Referenda are two-edged swords and may be used to compromise legislative prudence and weaken the effectiveness of the existing revenue management framework (Bell and Faria 2007).

Another way to reinforce the oil law is to adopt a constitutional amendment addressing certain key elements. A constitutional amendment would significantly strengthen the controls over the collection and use of oil revenues and would inhibit – but not prevent – the ability of any party or subdivision of the state to arbitrarily or unilaterally change the rules governing the oil account. In the unlikely event that an unconstitutional government attempts to seize power, such an amendment might also help protect the country from the seizure of funds, especially if the funds are held in an international institution outside of the country.

An amendment could reaffirm key principles of the oil revenue management law. For instance, the amendment might state that all petroleum resources and the revenues derived from them are the property of the state and cannot be pledged or encumbered, that all revenues from such resources must be deposited in the oil account, that all transfers from the oil account to the general funds of the Treasury must be approved by the appropriately designated institution or institutions, that the activities of the oil account, including all deposits and withdrawals, shall be public, that monies from the oil account can be made available only for particular specified uses and, possibly, that pledges or other encumbrances on the petroleum resources of the state are prohibited. The constitutional amendment could be passed separately or in conjunction with the oil law. Such amendments need to be carefully drafted so as not to be construed as creating a monopoly on drilling and production by the state.

Even though the government maintains full control of a fund, the stability of a fund could also be enhanced by the involvement of regional or international institutions such as the World Bank. Even where such institutions have simply observer status or non-voting membership, they can provide an additional degree of professionalism, transparency and accountability. Apart from enhancing management, their presence could be especially helpful in resisting domestic pressures driven by short-run political advantage.

Whatever form the fund takes, however, legislators and those assisting them must recognise that the law without strong supporting institutions may become just paper. In the end, popular support rather than good drafting is the most important sustaining mechanism, but a well-constructed law may help increase and build that support. There is a possibility of a virtuous circle in which a workable and effective law creates stronger popular constituencies who, in turn, will act to support and maintain the law.

Therefore, Guyana must manage its offshore operations effectively, since it is an important part of a holistic approach in ensuring that the most value is extracted for the benefits of the operators and the country. Hence, maximising economic rents from the petroleum resources should be the key objective of the government.

Consequently, with a current reserve of more than eight billion barrels of oiland more to be discovered, and with first oil delivered in 2019, Guyana mustdevelop a new growth model to transform the potential resource windfall into long-term prosperity. Such a model should have six core elements:

1. building the institutions and governance of the resources sector;

2. developing infrastructure;

3. ensuring robust fiscal policy and competitiveness;

4. supporting local content;

5. deciding how to spend a resources windfall wisely; and

6. transforming resource wealth into broader economic development.

Institutions and governance of the resources sector

There is a common view that a government has only two choices in the wayit participates in the resources sector: letting private-sector firms operate with minimal involvement from the state beyond taxation and regulation orcontrolling production through a state-owned company. However, the rangeof possible government roles is much wider than this, as the following examples illustrate:

- No state ownership: In Australia and Canada and elsewhere, the state does not have direct involvement in the industry but receives taxes, royalties, or both.

- Minority investor: The state has a minority stake in a company but does not play an active role in its management or direction.

- Majority-owned, with limited operatorship: The state has a majoritystake in a company and plays a role in the company's management, but less than 10 per cent of the company's production is operated by the state, or the state operates exclusively in certain segments such as onshore oil.

- Majority-owned operator: These companies are fully or majority-owned by the state, and more than 10 per cent of the company's production is operated by the state company.

- Government monopolist: Pemex in Mexico and Saudi Aramco in Saudi Arabia are fully owned by the state. Those and other companies in this category account for more than 80 per cent of the country's total production.

The popularity of each type of participation varies according to the resource. Today, more than half of oil and gas producers representing almost three-quarters of world production, are fully or majority state-owned (McKinsey Global Institute 2013). No single model of government participation works best in all countries – countries that have taken the same approach have experienced vastly different levels of success. The best approach depends on the context. Regardless of the model chosen, there are three guiding principles which are vital for Guyana's successful state participation.

First, the government needs to establish a stable regulatory regime with clearrules and well-defined roles for each player in the sector.

Second, it is important to ensure that there is competitive pressure by exposing national operators to private-sector competition, strongly benchmarking performance, or imposing other market disciplines such as scrutiny from private shareholders or bondholders.

Finally, the state needs to play a central role in attracting and retaining world-class talent into the sector – even more important if the state choosesto play a more active operational role.

Infrastructure

On average, resource-driven countries such as Guyana do not compare favourably with the rest of the world on their infrastructure, and this often puts investors off (Global Competitiveness Report 2012-2013). This could be particularly challenging given that capital markets are not well developed in many resource-driven countries. However, these economies can help to address the infrastructure imperative by transforming the productivity of infrastructure investment – in other words, they can do more with less. Therefore, Guyana can use three main levers that can help to obtain better infrastructural output: improving project selection and optimising infrastructure portfolios; streamlining delivery; and making the most of existing infrastructure, including sharing it.

The third area is an opportunity for the economy given the large infrastructure requirements of major extractive projects. Given the huge needs of the country, Guyana could look closely at ways of sharing infrastructure. By doing so, it can take advantage of private-sector capital and know-how; build stable, long-term partnerships with extractive companies; and achieve broader social benefits from the infrastructure that is put in place. Hence, the government must think carefully about their approach to resource-related infrastructure to ensure that it provides the maximum benefits to society.

Competitiveness and fiscal policy

Guyana has much to gain from doing all it can to ensure that the petroleum resource sectors are as globally competitive as possible. A robust resource industry creates jobs, contributes to a government's finances through tax and royalty payments and ensures sustained spending on exploration, increasing the viability of marginal deposits. National competitiveness becomes even more important as major new projects turn out to be more expensive and complex, and as greater volatility in resource prices increases the risk of projects being postponed or cancelled.

However, Guyana should not focus too narrowly on fiscal policy, without considering the broader competitiveness implications for its overall economy. In this context, focus should be on the resource's competitiveness, which encompasses three major elements of competitiveness: production costs, country risk, and the government 'take' (the share of revenue that accrues to the government).

This approach takes into account the real economics of projects, including a country's geology and factors such as the availability of infrastructure and regulatory or policy risks. Governments have the ability to affect all three of the elements of competitiveness including, of course, how much of the revenue pie they will take by setting royalties and taxes.

Production costs vary significantly relative to revenue depending on the type of resource and the geology of any particular asset. Costs (as a share of project revenue) are generally higher in mining than in oil and gas and for new sites. This demonstrates that the government take is closely correlated to production costs. In essence, when production costs are high, the government take is necessarily lower to ensure that costs are competitive with alternative investments.

This is true for individual resources and across resources. Whilst a government obviously cannot control factors such as the proximity of resource deposits to the coast, the quality of crude oil, or mineral grades, there are still avenues available to reduce capital and operating costs, especially by focusing on regulation, supply chains, productivity and co-operation with the industry.

Political or regulatory risk (measured as a share of the value of a project) can sometimes amount to a very high per cent of the value of the government take expressed as a percentage of revenue. This significantly weakens the competitiveness and attractiveness of the country. Even allowing for below optimal levels of government take, this demonstrates the importance of risk to companies.

Hence, there are large opportunities for Guyana to reduce risk by developing its ability to understand and negotiate contracts (ensuring that the contracts are fair and seen to be fair), adopting a set of formal legal mechanisms to help reassure investors and generally improving interaction with investors and companies.

Guyana will achieve far more by focusing on production costs and reducing risks in collaboration with resource companies than by narrowly focusing on trying to increase the government take. Successfully reducing production costs and risks produces a larger revenue pie that can then be shared by the government and the resource companies.

Local content development

Beyond generating taxes and royalties, the extractive industry can make substantial contributions to a country's economic development by supporting local employment and supply chains. Between 40 per cent and 80 per cent of the revenue created in oil and gas is spent on the procurement of goods and services, often exceeding tax and royalty payments in some cases. Increasing the proportion of goods and services that are procured locally ('local content') will be a key goal for policymakers in the resource-driven economy of Guyana. If the local content regulations are designed poorly, they can substantially reduce the competitiveness of the resources sector, endangering the jobs and investment that it brings, as well as violate free trade agreements. Regulation can, for instance, cause cost inflation or delay the execution of projects. Therefore, for a new and emerging oil and gas economy, Guyana should apply the following five fundamental principles to achieve effective local-content policies:

- Know where the value is and where the jobs are: The first imperative is for policymakers to gain detailed knowledge of the resources supply chain so that they understand where total value is in terms of revenue and employment.

- Understand the competitive edge: The spending that can be captured locally varies significantly among countries due to a number of factors, including the type of resource, the level of industrialisation, the country's unique aspects such as location and language, and whether other industries have a significant presence.

- Carefully assess the opportunity cost of regulatory intervention: When governments impose local-content requirements, they must carefully assess whether regulations are too unwieldy for companies, unnecessarily raising costs, potentially causing significant delays and damaging competitiveness. They should also guard against creating perverse incentives.

- Don't just regulate, enable: Most resource-driven countries devote too little attention to creating an environment that supports the achievement of local content targets. Government can assist in a number of areas, from helping to develop skills to providing financing and coordinating local suppliers.

- Carefully track and enforce progress: Making procedures simple to administer and track, appointing a credible regulator with enforcement power, and creating a regulatory body that can co-ordinate efforts are crucial to making progress on local content.

Private companies play an essential role in the development of local content. It is crucial for companies to have a detailed understanding of their future spending profile and the local supplier base; to organise effectively to achieve their local content goals by rooting them deeply in company processes for procurement and human resources rather than corporate social responsibility; to engage proactively with the government as they make local content policy decisions; and to support the development of local supply chains through targeted skill-building, and research and development programmes.

Policy implications

A key outcome for new petro-states such as Guyana is that a high degree of discretion by a single political constituency creates incentives to use up windfall revenues as soon as they come in instead of accumulating them. This relationship holds in practice as well as in theory. Hence, the optimal economic policies should not let year-to-year government expenditures vary much in response to oil revenue fluctuation. On average, there is no discernible pass-through of year-to-year oil revenue changes to aggregate government consumption. The coefficient on year-to-year changes in oil revenues is statistically indistinguishable from zero (Humphreys and Sandhu 2007).

Policymakers have strong political incentives not to follow what economists may describe as the economically best policy. Therefore, do not be very surprised to find that economic logic is rarely followed in natural resource- rich countries. Nevertheless, it can be in the interest of all parties, including incumbents, to find institutional arrangements that help discipline expenditure.

This shows that overspending can result from the fact that individual policymakers cannot commit to undertaking a given set of actions in the future. The practical issue is, then, how to overcome this problem. In particular, what kind of institutional reforms may improve the ability of policymakers to make mutually advantageous, credible commitments?

It is in light of this question that the decision whether or not to establish a Natural Resources Fund (NRF) – and what kind of fund to design – should be resolved. Since an NRF is not necessary for strictly economic reasons, the rationale for it has to be as a vehicle for institutional solutions to the political economy problem. If that is impossible, an NRF is at best useless – and if designed without a view to its effect on political incentives, may even make such incentives worse – and should be eschewed. Designers of prospective NRFs, therefore, must determine whether an NRF can realign local incentives. As has been emphasised, this is different from answering the basic economic question of what the optimal time path of natural resource finance expenditure would be. Instead, it is recommended that the focus should be on what the agents entrusted with carrying out the expenditure policy are likely to do, and how different NRF designs may change their behaviour. Such analysis could conceivably prefer an NRF that encouraged a less-than-perfect expenditure path, but a path that policymakers would, in fact, implement, to one which called for policymakers to implement the optimal policy but gave them no incentive to comply.

The best design will be different in different countries. It has to take account of the local political economy, which is best understood by experienced practitioners with intimate knowledge of local political conditions. Hence, at a general level, list the types of institutional mechanisms that could be implemented through an NRF, and that may work in some local settings, if not in all. The aim, then, is to provide an inventory of potential institutional 'fixes', which designers of NRFs can use as a roadmap to identify solutions that are most likely to work in their local political setting.

The ways in which NRFs could embody institutional solutions to the incentive problem fall, very roughly, into three categories:

1. The NRF can be set up with rules that govern the magnitude and composition of spending from it. The use of rules rather than discretionary decisions can provide one way of improving the regularity of policy across governments and help solve the commitment problem identified above.

2. An NRF can impose a separation or sharing of decision-making authority between different political constituencies. For example, the preceding discussion suggests that one way to remedy the commitment problem is to separate the authority to decide how much is to be spent from the authority to decide on what it is spent.

3. An NRF can have an informational role. It can be seen that under certain conditions, transparency increases the ability of the citizenry to hold the government accountable. In addition, it is well known from the economics of information that when information is scarce and asymmetric, efficient outcomes are more difficult to sustain. An NRF could alleviate this problem by facilitating the flow of information within the government system and between it and the population or the international public.

Spending the windfall

There is a broad range of approaches for Guyana to use resource revenues. It can invest the money abroad or use it to repay foreign debt. Guyana can also invest at least a portion of its oil revenue at home in infrastructure and other key areas. A share of revenue can be directed to specific regions for both investment and consumption purposes. The government can also use resources revenue more generally for domestic needs such as higher wages for public sector workers, subsidies for energy resources, or other social welfare programmes.

Whilst the best approach may vary somewhat, there are some valuable lessons from international experience to date that can be broadly applied. Guyana should consider the following if it wants to reap the full benefits of its resource endowments:

- Set expectations: To counter ill-informed pressure that could lead to wasteful spending, governments need to agree early in the process on the principles for how the resource wealth will be used and manage expectations among their citizens accordingly (Amoako-Tuffour 2011).

- Ensure spending is transparent and benefits are visible: Governments need to ensure that institutional mechanisms are put in place for a high level of transparency so that recipients see the benefits of invested resource windfalls.

- Smooth government expenditure: Setting a target for the non-commodity government budget balance can insulate public expenditures from volatility. During periods of relatively high commodity prices or output, the overall budget may accumulate a surplus, while during periods of low prices or output it may run a deficit but leave spending intact (International Monetary Fund 2009).

- Keep government lean: Resource-driven countries often suffer from bloated government bureaucracies. Such effects reduce not only public sector productivity but also incentives for working in the private sector, inhibiting wider economic development. Hence, Guyana should seek to keep the public sector in proportion by regularly comparing ratios for each function with those of other countries. It should also consider how it can consistently recognise duplicative structures in the public sector that could be consolidated. One method to keep pay consistent is to benchmark wages to similar jobs in the private sector and to assign public sector roles a 'clean wage' without hidden perks or privileges (McKinsey Center for Government 2012).

- Shift from consumption to investment: Channelling some of the resource wealth into domestic investment and savings is crucial to start transforming natural resource wealth into long-term prosperity. Establishing institutional mechanisms to support this process can be useful, because they can address any bias towards government consumption spending and deficits, enhance fiscal discipline, and raise the quality of debate and scrutiny.

- Boost domestic capabilities to use funds well: Resource-driven governments need to ensure the development of strong investment capabilities in the public sector. The International Monetary Fund (IMF) and the World Bank jointly produce an index of public investment efficiency, enabling countries to track progress in this area (Dabla-Norris et al. 2012). Some of the key areas to address include project appraisal, selection, implementation and auditing.

Economic development

Very few resource-driven countries have sustained strong Gross Domestic Product (GDP) growth for longer than a decade. Even those that have appeared to put their economics on a healthier longer-term growth trajectory have rarely managed to transform that growth into broader economic prosperity.

However, doing so is not impossible. One major imperative for Guyana is to focus on removing barriers to productivity across five key areas of the economy: the resources sector itself; resource rider sectors such as utilities and construction; manufacturing; local services such as retail trade and financial services; and agriculture.

Local services, which include hospitality, telecommunications and financial sectors, are often seen as the indirect beneficiaries of the resource booms. These sectors can achieve large productivity improvements, which can often result in significant growth in GDP and employment, but these sectors are often overlooked by policymakers. Removing microeconomic barriers can significantly increase productivity and economic growth for an emerging economy such as Guyana.

Transparency: scope of public information

The requirement of transparency and the establishment of mechanisms that ensure such transparency are critical in any oil revenue management law. As a general rule, all oil revenue-related information should be made public. Any law should provide a non-exhaustive list of items subject to transparency, and the parties responsible for making each piece of information public.

Among many international efforts to foster and strengthen transparency in natural resource management are the Natural Resource Governance Institute and the Extractive Industries Transparency Initiative (EITI) campaigns, both of which support transparency of resource revenues through the disclosure of information on natural resource-related payments made by private companies to resource exporting governments, among others. Also, of particular note and value is the International Monetary Fund (IMF) Guide on Resource Revenue Transparency published in 2005.

A special issue with respect to the publication of payment data is whether such information should be available on an individual company basis or should be aggregated. In countries with mature institutions, individual company data may be available, but in many emerging countries such as Guyana, there is no such disclosure. While aggregate data may be the best information available in some countries, civil society or parliamentarians cannot use such data to compare directly payment data reported by the government with payments reported by the companies.

The local Oil Revenue Law may take the preferred approach and mandates public access to individual payment data rather than to summaries or aggregations of information. Further, there could be a national declaration of principles requiring public disclosure of individual company data and of contracts by the governing authority and the companies. One of the advantages of having direct public web access to the records of the custodial account is that payment information is available on a disaggregated basis and, without any intervention or discretionary action by the government, that all of the information can be made available to other branches of the government, civil society and interested international groups.

A separate issue is the publication of all oil-related contracts. Although governmental oil contracts have traditionally been kept confidential in the developing world, that is not the practice in advanced democracies. Moreover, the most recent practice even in developing countries is moving toward disclosure. For instance, the local oil revenue management law could require disclosure and public access to 'all contracts relating to the participation of the state, or any enterprise or entity owned or controlled in whole or in part by the state, the scope of which directly or indirectly concerns activities related to oil resources or oil revenues'.

Making contracts public ensures the integrity of bidding and negotiations, which, in turn, ensures that awards are made competitively and are consistent with whatever rules have been laid down. Without the transparency of contractual agreements, it is impossible for civil society or interested members of parliament to ensure that contracts are enforced, and payments made accordingly. Making contracts public when they are entered makes possible full public oversight of those agreements that will be central to the political economy of the country in the future and is the only way to give such contracting full political legitimacy. This legitimacy is important not only for the citizenry but also for the companies because it provides protection against political second-guessing when exploration prospects turn out favourably. Secrecy may protect the negotiators (government and private), but no one has identified a governmental interest in keeping agreements private. The contracts themselves are shared among industry partners; it is only the public that is excluded if they are kept confidential.

Sometimes in order not to make contracts or payments public, companies rely on confidentiality clauses and assert that it is the government that prevents them from making such information public. However, the government can and should, in the exercise of its own sovereign power, determine that such information shall be publicly disclosed. Certainly, a self-imposed confidentiality argument has no weight in the debate on a forward-looking law.

Any exceptions to the disclosure requirements should be very narrowly drawn. The local oil revenue management law could specifically allow the withholding of information only if it is classified as confidential by law or treaty, and it puts the burden of claiming confidentiality on the proponent. The local law must protect proprietary information from disclosure, but specifically prohibits making any payment information confidential.

References

Joe Amoako-Tuffour (2011) Public Participation in the Making of Ghana's Petroleum Revenue Management Law [Homepage of Natural Resource Charter Technical Advisory Group]. https://resourcegovernance.org/sites/default/files/documents/ghana -public- participation.pdf, accessed on 24 February 2019

John A P Chandler (2018) Petroleum Resource Management: How Governments Manage Their Offshore Petroleum Resources, Cheltenham,UK: Edward Elgar Publishing

Era Dabla-Norris, Jim Brumby, Annette Kyobe, et al. (2012) Investing in public investment: An index of public investment efficiency, Journal of EconomicGrowth, Vol. 17, No. 3 pp 235-266

Richard Dobbs, Jeremy Oppenheim, Adam Kendall, Fraser Thompson, Martin Bratt, and Fransje van der Marel (2013) Reverse the Curse: Maximizing the Potential of Resource-driven Economies [Homepage of McKinsey Global Institute]. https://www.mckinsey.com/industries/metals-and-mining/our-insights/reverse-the-curse-maximizing-the-potential-of-resource-driven-economies, accessed on 25 February 2019

Biniam Gebre, Petter Hallman, Mark Minukas, and Becca O'Brien (2012) Transforming Government Performance Through Lean Management [Homepage of McKinsey Centre for Government]. https://www.mckinsey.com/~/media/mckinsey/dotcom/client_servi ce/PublicSector/PDFS/MCG_Transforming_through_lean_manage ment.ashx, accessed on 25 February 2019

Andrea Schaechter, Carlos Caceres, Xavier Debrun, et al. (2009) Fiscal Rules: Anchoring Expectations for Sustainable Public Finances [Homepage of International Monetary Fund].

https://www.imf.org/external/np/pp/eng/2009/121609.pdf

Klaus Schwab (2012) The Global Competitiveness Report 2012-
2013 [Homepage of World Economic Forum].
https://www.weforum.org/reports/global-competitiveness-report-
2012- 2013, accessed on 23 February 2019

About the contributor

In 2019 Bobby Gossai Jr. was pursuing the Degree of Doctor of
Philosophy in Economics at the University of Aberdeen with a
research focus on 'Fiscal Policies and Regulations for an Emerging
Petroleum Producing Country in a Volatile Price Environment'. He
completed his MSc (Econ) in Petroleum, Energy Economics and
Finance from the same institution, and also holds an   MSC in
Economics from the University of the West Indies. His professional
experiences include being the head of the Guyana Oil and Gas
Association and senior policy analyst and advisor at the Ministry of
Natural Resources and Environment. Today, in 2022, he is the senior
petroleum co-ordinator for the government of Guyana.

SECTION FOUR: LESSONS FROM NEAR AND AFAR

Introduction

John Mair

As Guyana goes from nothing to world oil power in a decade what can the country learn from others with oil riches? In this section we look at the experiences in five other oil 'kingdoms': two near neighbours, Trinidad and Tobago, and Venezuela, then Scotland, Ghana, and Texas.

'Dax' Driver, from the Trinidad and Tobago Energy Chamber, gives an up-to-date picture of what Guyana can learn from his country in a piece specially written for this book. The Trinis, whose oil and gas is running out and who have closed their refinery, look enviously to Guyana for their future Trinidad oil 'experts', and businesses are already starting to colonise the Guyana oil scene – not without demur. Driver offers five lessons from Trinidad and Tobago's century of oil. In his words: 'Trinidad and Tobago have many lessons it can offer to Guyana, the world's most exciting new hydrocarbon province. This includes both things to emulate and things to avoid'.

In a piece from 2019 Simon Flowers, chief analyst at Wood Mackenzie, looked at the lessons Guyana could learn from its fractious neighbour, the Bolivar Republic of Venezuela. That has the biggest reserves of oil in the world, though its activities have been somewhat constrained by US sanctions. In 'Lessons from Venezuela (2019)', he counselled Guyana to avoid over-dependence on oil. 'It's a window to a dystopian future for Guyana, he warned. 'Building infrastructure and raising education standards will facilitate development of other sectors. Local content and employment requirements for the oil industry can support this process.'

My own long-term interest in Guyana oil was the spur for this book's four previous editions. In this fifth edition of the book I explore some more lessons that Guyana could learn from Venezuela.I look at how quickly Venezuela went from being a petro power state to a poor pariah state. The lessons for Guyana are as much geopolitical as economic.

Earlier in this book Tulsi Dyal Singh outlined his view of the bright future for Oil Dorado. His oil present is quite rosy: he has oil under his land in the Texas Permian Basin, and that generates a nice monthly royalty. Tulsi has been on the board of the Renovar Energy Corporation for 17 years and chaired an oil bank in Texas as well. He knows oil. Here, in 'Lessons from Midland Texas', he looks from his adopted home to his mother's land: 'It must be an exciting time for those living in Guyana. Such promise of a better life for all, in potentially such a short time. Such luck, such opportunity!'

Finally, I take a look at the lessons Guyana could learn from Ghana.

So, there are plenty of templates – positive and negative – from round the world for Oil Dorado to follow or to avoid.

They decide.

Chapter Twenty-Two

Five lessons for Guyana from Trinidad and Tobago (2022)

Thackwray (Dax) Driver, President and CEO of the Energy Chamber of Trinidad and Tobago, offers the lessons of his country's hundred years of experience in oil and gas to its neighbour, the world's most exciting new hydrocarbon province

Trinidad and Tobago is one of the world's oldest hydrocarbon producers, with commercial oil production starting in 1908 and commercial gas production starting in 1953. With over a century of experience, Trinidad and Tobago has many lessons it can offer to Guyana, the world's most exciting new hydrocarbon province. This includes both things to emulate and things to avoid.

1. Remain open to international investors

Trinidad and Tobago has always been open to direct foreign investment in its hydrocarbon industry. While state-owned companies play an important role, Trinidad and Tobago has avoided the temptation to expropriate foreign-owned assets and has carefully guarded its reputation for respecting the sanctity of contracts and adhering to investment agreements. This has been a major strength for the country and has meant that investors have remained confident in investing in the country, even though our resource base has not been as impressive as some others.

There have been times when the agreements signed with foreign investors did not, with hindsight, turn out to give the best possible value to Trinidad and Tobago. In those cases, the government has sometimes sought to renegotiate but this must always be done by mutual consent and not unilaterally imposed. Contracts have an end-date and governments have an opportunity to renegotiate at the end of contract periods. Once investors lose trust in a jurisdiction it is very difficult to win it back. Expropriation of assets and unilateral imposition of new contracts may be politically popular in the short-term, but it inevitably ends in disaster.

2. Make decisions quickly when things change

The international energy industry is always in a state of flux. Technology and markets always change and can change quickly. Trinidad and Tobago's liquefied natural gas (LNG) industry was built in the 1990s and 2000s on the demand for imported gas in the United States. The 'shale gas revolution', based on the application of fracking technology, totally changed the shape of the gas industry and the US is now the world's leading LNG exporter. As the global industry changes, countries must shift their strategy and change their policies and regulations.

While we have generally been able to change our approach as the global industry has changed, we have sometimes been slow to take decisions. For example, Trinidad and Tobago has been slow to make changes to the windfall taxation system for crude oil production put in place in 1981 during the first oil boom. This windfall tax was designed to kick in when oil prices averaged above US$50 per barrel as a way of ensuring a fair share of revenue for the government. Unfortunately, the threshold price was not inflation-linked and the windfall tax still kicks in at $50, which is certainly not considered high today. This has acted as a disincentive to investment in crude oil production and has significantly contributed to the decline in activity and oil production over the past two decades (the tax is not levied against natural gas). While the issue associated with this tax has been identified repeatedly, it has been difficult to amend a system which delivers short-term revenue to the government, even though it dampens long-term investment.

While the industry in Guyana has a very rosy future at present, the government should always be ready to quickly make decisions if circumstances change. Being able to respond quickly to changing circumstances is important to long-term success. This means having nimble and responsive policy-making systems within the government.

3. Invest in training and skills development

Trinidad and Tobago has invested heavily in education, training, and skills development. This has created a cadre of skilled leaders, professionals, technicians, and skilled workers. While the energy sector has always been open to international investors and international service companies and contractors, most workers in the industry are nationals or permanent residents. The Energy Chamber tracks the nationality of all workers in the petrochemical, LNG, and heavy industrial sector (through our administration of the basic safety assessments for all workers). In 2021, 99 per cent of the workers in this sub-sector were Trinidad and Tobago nationals or permanent residents. This has been consistent since we started tracking the nationality of workers a decade ago, with around 16,000 individuals per annum undergoing the assessment.

The University of the West Indies has produced a lot of the leaders in the energy industry, including many petroleum engineers and geologists, but also lawyers, accountants, and other professionals. Many other leaders went to international universities on government scholarships before returning to Trinidad. More recently, the University of Trinidad and Tobago has produced many graduates with strong practical experience and skills, filling important managerial and technical roles.

Historically, many skilled labourers came out of company apprentice systems and the skilled technicians and craft workers produced through these programmes formed the backbone of the industry during the 1970s, 1980s, and 1990s. With the shift to more services being contracted out to service companies, more of the skilled labour force has come through institutions such as the NESC Technical Institute and the Kenson School of Production Technology. Service companies and contractors have also often developed robust in-house training programmes.

One area in which we could have done more in training and development is in the adoption of competency-based assessments that provide certification for skilled workers who have learned on the job. There are many skilled workers who do not possess the certificates to show that they are competent, and this hampers their ability to move up in organisations or to work internationally. This is an area in which Guyana and Trinidad and Tobago could cooperate for mutual benefit and ensure that as workers gain practical skills, they also get competency-based certification against the Caribbean Vocational Qualification (CVQ) system.

Nevertheless, the investments that Trinidad and Tobago has made in education and skills development means that we do have many nationals working in the oil and gas industry outside of the country. You would be hard-pressed to find an oilfield or an LNG facility anywhere in the world without a Trinidadian working there. Of course, there are many skilled and experienced Trinidadians now working in Guyana.

4. Invest in creating a safety culture

Trinidad and Tobago's energy sector has developed a robust safety culture and the safety record in the industry has generally been good, though this cannot ever lead to complacency. The safety performance of many of the offshore operators and downstream process facilities has compared well in international benchmarking exercises.

The safety culture within the energy sector has developed in a context of generally weak national safety regulatory enforcement and industry leaders have had to work hard to keep a strong focus on safety in this environment. Through the Safe to Work programme (STOW), the Energy Chamber has played a role in developing the industry safety culture with a particular focus on contractor safety management. This award-winning scheme has created an industrywide uniform HSE pre-qualification programme with over 2,200 audits having been conducted and 750 companies having been certified against the STOW requirements.

STOW has shown how industry standards can help build a strong safety culture through industry self-regulation, rather than having to rely on regulation from the state. These experiences can be easily transferred to Guyana.

5. Be very careful with subsidies

Like many other hydrocarbon-producing economies, Trinidad and Tobago has shielded citizens from international fuel and electricity prices through subsidies. This means that citizens have enjoyed some of the world's cheapest electricity rates with gasoline and diesel prices typically at much lower rates than in other Caribbean countries. LPG or cooking gas has also been heavily subsidised and is very cheap compared with most countries.

While citizens obviously benefit from these subsidised prices (though surprisingly still often complain) the subsidy system has led to some serious distortions and poor social, economic, and environmental outcomes. When the transport fuel subsidy was originally set up it was to be paid for through a levy on oil companies, but as car ownership and hence fuel use increased and then, as oil production decreased, the government had to step in to pay for the subsidy directly from central government funds. Over the decades, billions of dollars of government funds have gone into keeping fuel prices low. This is effectively a transfer of funds to better-off households, who typically own more than one private motor vehicle and who use most fuel.

The subsidy has also led to high levels of car ownership and debilitating traffic jams that seriously affect people's mental and physical health and national productivity. With the benefit of hindsight, if the billions of dollars of funding for gasoline and diesel had instead been funnelled into investments in public transport, Trinidad and Tobago would have had a world-class public transport system and a healthier and happier population. Having created the current system, however, it is very difficult and politically unpopular to implement a new model for mobility. Guyana would do well to avoid this problem in the first place by not subsidising transport fuels and investing heavily in public transport.

Trinidad and Tobago's electricity is almost 100 per cent produced by natural gas power generation. The electricity subsidy is effectively provided by the gas industry, who are contractually obligated to provide a tranche of gas at prices well below market rates to that sector. This gas for electricity accounts for about 10 per cent of current total gas production. With very low electricity prices, the population is typically not very conscious of wasting electricity and a lot of energy is wasted. Trinidad and Tobago is very energy-inefficient. This means that gas that could be channelled to export-earning sectors like LNG, methanol, or ammonia is instead simply wasted.

There are excellent social and economic reasons for ensuring that every single household can access electricity as well as a good argument for making this available at a subsidised rate. It makes sense to subsidise the small amount of electricity needed for lights, a fridge, and a fan or two. It does not make sense to subsidise flat-screen TVs, central air conditioning, and pool pumps for the richest households. It is the richest households who use most of the electricity and it is these households who should be incentivised to be more energy-efficient, by making sure that they pay market prices for their electricity.

Smart meters mean that it is easy to put in a place a rate system along these lines and Guyana should be investing heavily in its grid and metering system, at the same time as it is embarking on its gas-to-electricity project. Once subsidies are implemented across the board, they are politically very difficult to remove, and Guyana would do well to avoid this problem in the first place.

There are, of course, many other lessons that Guyana could learn from Trinidad and Tobago and the Energy Chamber is always open to sharing our knowledge and understanding. Our countries and energy industries are closely intertwined, and I am sure that we will also have a lot to learn from Guyana, as the Guyanese oil industry continues its unprecedented rise.

About the contributor

Dr Thackwray Driver, better known as Dax, has been the President and CEO of the Energy Chamber of Trinidad and Tobago for the past twenty years. He oversaw the transformation of the organisation from a regional chamber in South Trinidad to a national trade association representing companies from across the energy value chain, from small family-owned contractors through to major multi-nationals and state-owned oil and gas companies. He has a PhD in environmental history from the University of London.

Chapter Twenty-Three

Lessons from Venezuela (2019)

Venezuela's slide from top of the heap to a virtual bit player in the oil market is a slow-motion car crash. Production sank progressively from 2.6m. barrels per day (b/d) a decade ago, when it was third in Opec behind only Saudi Arabia and Iran, to 2m. b/d by Q3 2017. Decline since has been precipitous. Today it's just 1.1m b/d, says Simon Flowers, in an article originally published in Forbes, in 2019

The market has shrugged off the loss, even with the absence of sanctioned Iranian oil. Venezuela's heavy barrels have been largely displaced by supplies from Canada, Mexico and elsewhere.

As the US sanctions announced 28 January bite, worse lies ahead. Two factors will drive production down to 0.7m. b/d over the next six months in our latest forecasts: lack of access to the diluent needed to help the heavy crude flow; and limited availability of finance for workovers and basic maintenance on wells. The intensifying economic squeeze and external political pressure will likely lead to a new government and stabilisation in 2020. Then, perhaps, recovery can begin.

The collapse of the economy has been one of the most severe (barring wars) since the fall of the Soviet Union. Six years ago, GDP per person was US$14,500, placing Venezuela just behind Chile as the wealthiest economy in South America and in the top 50 globally. In the past five years, the size of the economy has roughly halved. Besides severe recession, the country is grappling with hyperinflation and a population exodus.

A central factor in the shrivelling of the economy has been over-dependence on oil. Non-oil industries have all but vanished, their share of exports falling from around 25 per cent in the late 1990s to less than 3 per cent in recent years. The government borrowed heavily against rising oil revenues in the previous decade, fuelling social spending. When oil prices fell in 2014, Venezuela had minimal savings and no other buffer. The result has been a shortage of dollars to pay for imports of even basic goods, never mind repaying its international creditors or maintaining oil production. It's a window to a dystopian future for Guyana. Venezuela's neighbour to the east, Guyana is developing its first offshore oil and gas finds made in the past four years. There's a growing number of them. Production could exceed 1m b/d, putting Guyana in non-Opec's top ten – from nowhere. Operator ExxonMobil's plan for the Liza complex will transform the economy.

Guyana's GDP was $3.7bn (all figures in US dollars) in 2017 but will grow by multiples. Our analysis of the upstream project assumes total investment of over $30bn; plateauing at $5bn annually in the early 2020s as the known discoveries are developed; all perhaps matched by investment down the value chain onshore. Tax revenues kick in from the mid-2020s and build up quickly to more than $10bn a year. For such a small economy, the scale of development is staggering. Assuming oil production of 1m b/d by 2030, Guyana's output per person will be higher than any other major oil producer. A four-fold increase in the size of its economy over a decade is possible, catapulting Guyana into the high-income bracket. Azerbaijan and Equatorial Guinea are other countries in recent history that have experienced similar explosive growth, but from a lower base.

What can Guyana do to make the most of its oil and avoid the pitfalls? Kuwait and the UAE have consistently invested a portion of revenues in sovereign wealth funds. Each had built up a buffer three to four times the size of their economies to draw on when the oil price collapsed in 2014. Such a strategy helps smooth out the boom-and-bust but requires a high degree of discipline. It will be tempting to spend, spend, spend. Another clear lesson from Venezuela is not to become too dependent on a single source of revenue. Building infrastructure and raising education standards will facilitate development of other sectors. Local content and employment requirements for the oil industry can support this process.

It will be a delicate balancing act. The role of government is also central to success in setting clear energy policy, establishing firm and independent regulation, and a stable fiscal policy. These set a framework for close collaboration with international operators. The fate of Venezuela is all the incentive needed to get this right.

About the contributor

Simon Flowers is chief analyst and chairman of Wood Mackenzie. He has more than 20 years of experience in the oil, gas, utilities and mining sectors, working with the boards of many energy companies on strategic issues. His views on major industry issues are regularly sought by the media in Europe, the US, and Asia. Simon graduated in geology from the University of Edinburgh, and worked for two years as a geologist in the oil industry in the Netherlands and offshore Egypt. He is based in Edinburgh.

Chapter Twenty-Four
Lessons from Venezuela (2023)

They have the biggest oil reserves in the world. But the lessons of the last two decades have not all been good ones. John Mair argues that Venezuela has gone from petro power state to poor pariah state

Guyana shares a disputed border with the Bolivar Republic of Venezuela. It is a fractious relationship. Put simply, Venezuela has laid claim to a third of Guyana for the last century and more. That case is currently before the International Court of Justice in the Hague.

Before 2015, Guyana was also the poor oil neighbour of the Bolivar republic.

Venezuela in South America is at the mercy of faraway geopolitics. Made by the USA, then unmade by them, then 'saved' by Russia, and now in process of being 'saved' anew by Uncle Sam, all thanks to Russia's 2022 invasion of Ukraine and the West being desperate for new energy sources.

In the beginning, Venezuela was fully qualified to become a titan of the global oil industry. One of the founding members of the Organization of the Petroleum Exporting Countries (OPEC), the South American nation holds the largest crude oil reserves in the world, amounting to more than 300bn barrels.
With an annual crude oil production of more than three million barrels per day, Venezuela was once, along with Mexico, one of the two largest oil-producing countries in Latin America. Eight per cent of their exports were oil, and that figure rose to a whopping 96 per cent in 2013.

It was a country based on oil: huge amounts, mainly exported to the USA. Surely nothing could go wrong, could it?

The socialist revolution

They called it the Bolivar Revolution in honour of the nineteenth-century national hero Simón Bolivar. Hugo Chavez seized power in the 1999 army coup and, on his death in 2013, his successor Nicholas Maduro imposed their brand of harsh socialism on the country. The oil industry was nationalised and much more too. The rich fled, mainly to the USA. Florida is Caracas in exile. Venezuela went from hero to zero in the eyes of the USA,

Chavez's version of socialism may have been popular with the struggling masses in what had been a very unequal society but it became a rogue state to the USA, especially to the very right-wing Trump regime from 2016. They accused the Maduro regime of fiddling elections and even went as far as to recognise the Opposition leader Juan Gaudio as the 'real' President in 2019.

Nevertheless, gradually increasing economic sanctions imposed by the US government since 2017 put further strains on Venezuela's oil sector. Where the US had previously been the leading destination for Venezuelan oil exports, by mid-2019 trade with them came to a complete halt.

The sector was kept going as a long-distance satellite of Putin's Russia and various contra deals in the Caribbean as part of the Petro Caribe strategy. Guyana, for example, traded rice for oil.

How far did they fall?

Nowadays, however, after nearly two decades of persistent decline in output, the country has dropped to fourth-biggest producer in the region, overtaken by Brazil and Colombia. In early 2022, Venezuela's monthly crude output reached an average of 700 thousand barrels of oil per day. While this represented a year-on-year growth, production had declined by more than 70 percent in comparison with output a decade earlier.

Venezuelan refinery production has dipped below 200 thousand barrels per day in the past three years, roughly fifteen per cent of its refining capacity. As a result, shortages of fuels such as gasoline (for years heavily subsidized by the government and considered by its citizens a birthright) have become a constant struggle. Petroleum is such an important lifeline for the nation that, even with the continual drop in production, Venezuela still managed to maintain an average of 1.7m daily barrels of crude oil exports for most of the decade.

In addition to allegations of rigging the 2020 election, Maduro's government has been accused of crimes against humanity, including the authorising of gruesome torture and extrajudicial killings, according to a 2020 report from the United Nations human rights body. Previous rounds of negotiations between Maduro and his opposition have fallen through, including most recent attempts in Oct. 2021.

Venezuela was seemingly on its uppers. There were food queues but Maduro was still firmly in power.

Then came the invasion of Ukraine

As the result of economic sanctions aimed at forcing Maduro out of power, US companies have been prohibited from conducting business with Venezuela's state-owned oil company since 2019 but he remains President.

Talks between the US and Venezuela governments began in March 2022. This was one month after Russia's invasion of Ukraine as President Joe Biden began searching for alternatives to Russian oil and the US looked to weaken Russia's economy as the war dragged on.

The Biden administration granted a licence in November 2022 to Chevron to resume oil production in Venezuela, easing sanctions imposed on the country in 2019 over corruption and human rights concerns. This licence comes with several limitations, however, including a provision prohibiting Chevron from conducting any transactions with Iran or Russian-owned entities in Venezuela. It also prohibits the country's nationalised oil company, Petroleos de Venezuela, S.A., which the US sanctioned in 2019, from receiving profits from Chevron's oil sales, which are intended to go instead to repaying debts owed to Chevron.

The lessons for Guyana

So from petro power state to poor pariah state and now in by the back door, the lesson for Guyana from Venezuela is always keep on the right side of the big Eagle to the north. The Bear is not a substitute any more. This is the new Monroe Doctrine. Guyana seems to have learned that lesson and is hugger-mugger with the USA and ExxonMobil. The USA resolved the 2020 election 'fiddling' crisis in favour of the current government and US Ambassador Sarah Lynch is one of the more respected voices in the country.

Chapter Twenty-Five

Lessons from Midland, Texas (2022)

Tulsi Dyal Singh, MD, lives in the Permian Basin, in Texas – the biggest-producing oilfield in the world. He was born in Guyana, which soon will be up there with Texas in the Oil Premier League

Booms and busts are real. Busts occur often. They are unexpected and unpredictable. They are devastating for most. Booms are just as frequent. Luck is as important as knowledge, skills, and timing.

I arrived in Midland, Texas, forty-three years ago. Midland sits on top of the middle of the Permian Basin, currently the most prolific producing oilfield in the world since it passed Saudi Arabia's Ghawar field three years ago. In May 2022, the Permian Basin produced 5.5m barrels of oil per day. Total production worldwide is 100m barrels per day.

I found Midland by accident. I knew nothing about oil. I was simply looking for a medium-sized city that was growing and needed medical doctors to come and open their private practice to take care of the increasing population. I was told that the reason for the increasing population was the rapid growth in the oil business but that mostly went over my head.

My initiation into oil and gas

But oil quickly gets into your blood. Within the first year, I was introduced to oil and gas investing by some of my patients and neighbours. I invested in four small drilling programmes. Two were dry holes right from the start. The other two were good wells, at least initially, but when a sudden crash in oil prices occurred less than two years later the wells became unprofitable. That was just the beginning. The local economy collapsed. Several established businesses closed. Many companies and individuals went bankrupt. For me, it was an abrupt, unwelcome, comprehensive, but eventually a cathartic education about booms and busts. The bright side was that some people survived. I was among them. But what an education it was. There was a bumper sticker that I saw that captured a widely held sentiment: 'Dear God, please send us another oil boom and I promise not to piss it off this time'.

Booms and busts are part of the oil and gas business. I have lived through several cycles. Many newcomers to the business believe that they can outsmart the commodity cycle. I have heard many novices and some who have been burnt before lecturing me on why each current boom is different from all the previous ones. They preen that the current party will never stop for the people who really know what they are doing. Few of those people are still around.

Permian Basin – hidden 'black gold, even under my lawn!

The Permian Oil Basin is all around me. The oil and gas zones are deep underground but the drilling rigs, the pump jacks, the tank batteries, the risers, the ubiquitous tanker trucks, the pipeline markers, the flare stacks, and the myriad other paraphernalia that enable the industry are on the surface, nearby, palpable and visible. But even though there is oil being produced from under my yard and there is a gas pipeline traversing my property, you will not see any of them. The production well runs horizontally, and it is two miles beneath my land surface and the pump jack and tank battery that support them are a mile and a half away. The gas pipeline is six feet below my lawn. It is made of steel. I know not to dig in its vicinity.

Booms always good?

Booms create massive amounts of activities and opportunities. The flood of money brings in lots of new people. Higher-paying oilfield jobs lure people away from lower-paying jobs especially in the service industries. Housing prices escalate and the cost of living often rises accompanying the oil prices upwards. For most of the people who ride each cycle up and then down the net benefit is marginal. For those who have royalties coming in or are owners or operators of a piece of the business the financial rewards can be astounding. I have seen US billionaires created within a year!

The pluses and minuses of oil

There is no other way to say it: the production of oil and gas and the consumption of oil and gas are severely hazardous to the environment and to the long-term liveability on planet Earth. For over a century, cheap, efficient, portable, widely available oil and gas have enabled mankind to master the universe like in no century before. But it's mostly unmitigated use so far has set us on the path of destroying our environment. The transition to renewable sources of energy such as wind, solar, hydro, and tidal, while capturing and sequestering a large portion of the carbon dioxide already in the atmosphere, are essential global priorities.

Money influences behaviour, at all levels of culture, perhaps especially at the level of corporate culture. I expect that there will be a flood of taxpayers' money diverted to carbon capture and carbon sequestration and that the corporations receiving the bulk of it will be the ones who caused it in the first place and who for years denied that there was a problem with carbon dioxide in the atmosphere. Money influences behaviour!

What can Guyana expect and how to salute the past?

It must be an exciting time for those living in Guyana. Such promise of a better life for all, in potentially such a short time. Such luck, such opportunity! I hope that my call from more than four years ago 'to all concerned to save the records, pictures, photographs, contracts, surveys, seismic studies, articles, analyses, economic proformas, engineering models, equipment replicas, invitations, press releases, drilling logs, core specimens, samples of first oil, in short everything related to the development of the oil and gas industry so that future generations can relive the current excitement in a future Guyana Petroleum Museum, Library and Hall of Fame' has seen action.

A message from my adopted land to the land of my motherland.

About the contributor

Tulsi Dyal Singh, MD, was born in Palymyra, Berbice, Guyana. He now lives in Midland, Texas, US. Both are or will be oil hot spots.

Chapter Twenty-Six
Lessons from Ghana

Guyana is trying to learn from other petro-states and their mistakes, among them Ghana in West Africa. John Mair takes a close look at the Ghanaian experience

Vice-president (and former President) Bharat Jagdeo, the de facto Guyana 'oil supremo', led a Guyana fact-finding delegation to Ghana in October 2021 to pick the brains of Ghanian key players. The traffic of expertise across the Middle Passage has been busy ever since. The President of Ghana, Nana Akufo-Addo, came to Georgetown in February 2022 to address the First International Energy conference. Many others have followed in his slipstream -- lawyers and tech experts and more. Branch offices have sprouted in Georgetown.

Does Ghana have anything to teach Guyana on oil? Well, the answer is both yes and no.

Good news

On the positive side, Ghana is a decade and more ahead. They discovered oil in 2007. Since then, they have benefited to the tune of $US1bn each year. Guyana has achieved that amount in 2022 and is only just at the beginning of their entrance to the field.

In 2019, Ghana was said to have the fastest-growing economy in the world. It was also praised for the steps it took to improve the regulation of the industry. Ghana was seen as a champion of growth for other nations within the continent and further afield to follow.

All was rosy but . . .

Not so good news

But, and there are plenty of buts, Ghana is still plagued with the social problems of poverty, unemployment, illiteracy, drift to the cities, encroachment on the forests and more. Oil wealth has not solved that.

Worst of all they seem to be running out of money to pay their international debts. Ghana is in debt distress. In December 2002 their Ministry of Finance announced that they were unable to meet their obligations on international loans, whether Eurobonds, bilateral, of any other stripe. In their words: 'The combination of adverse external shocks (the Ukraine war, Covid, etc.) has exposed Ghana to a surge in inflation, a large exchange rate depreciation, and stress on the financing of the budget. These factors taken together have put the sustainability of our debt at risk'.

In simple language, the piggy bank is empty.

From oil hero to oil zero

How did they get to this sorry state? Bad business. Political inter-party and intra-party interference in the oil industry has not always been good. When the party in power changes, oil companies exploit the vacuum.

The petroleum sector continues to be manipulated by politicians. This is done through the indiscriminate removal and appointment of technocrats and executives. The Ghana National Petroleum Corporation, the supposed regulator, has become notorious for being embroiled in several petroleum agreement scandals. Potentially, these are costing the Ghanaian taxpayer billions of dollars. There's still a lack of transparency and inadequate political will to propose and implement laws to the letter.

Recent revelations show that Ghana risks losing about US$1.5bn annually due to a 2020/21 gas supply agreement. The agreement has seen Ghana selling gas at a needlessly discounted rate of 77 per cent to a private entity. Ghana now has a surplus of gas.

The Petroleum Corporation had the mandate for petroleum exploration as well as imports of petroleum products for domestic consumption. Fiscal space was constrained at one time. Accordingly, one of the corporation's strategies was to use anticipated proceeds from future oil production from some fields to hedge oil price hikes. It also used proceeds from the sale of cocoa on the world market to directly pay for imported crude oil without having to look for foreign exchange to cover the cost.

These kinds of derivative transactions cost Ghana millions of dollars due to ill-informed advice from its financial advisers.

Contracts (production agreements) not sufficiently well enforced

In January 2023 the Africa Centre for Energy Policy (ACEP) produced an investigative report on Ghana which shows that it lost over US$882m on fourteen petroleum contracts since regulators failed to be vigilant. In their findings the investigative group described how the sixteen contracts it examined were signed in the period between 2006 and 2019. These contracts included specific deliverables to ensure that companies did not merely hold onto the blocks but instead proceeded to exploration and production.

The production agreements (PAs) gave companies between six and seven years for exploration, with this timeframe divided into three stages. A company is supposed to meet the minimum requirement for one stage as a prerequisite before moving to the next phase. Failure to perform minimum obligations incurs a sanction in a form of payment to the state.

The ACEP report explained that the investment requirements for just fourteen active PAs add up to a total of US$923m. Companies whose initial period has expired should have invested about US$750m in exploration. ACEP said the limited activity points to less than 2 per cent of the required minimum expenditure over the period, leaving Ghana losing out on over US$882m.

So, should Guyana send the Ghanaians back?

The legions of Ghanaian experts who have decamped to Georgetown may be bringing advice and experience but not all of it is positive. It is up to the Guyanese to sort the wheat from the chaff on that.

Rainforest Interlude

Grace Nichols

Nothing then, put to seek refuge
from the chaos of Stabroek Market Square
and the melting gold of the El Dorado-sun
and dive into the cool ambiance
of the Georgetown Museum – surfacing
among the glass cabinets of its stilled creation
drawn from the artistry of forest trees and rivers.
Like walking swimmers, we reacquaint with
Aripiama world's biggest fresh water fish,
Great Harpy-eagle, the startling, Hoatzin bird
and standing where my childhood left him,
old gold-seeking, gold-toothed, Pork-knocker,
saucepan and cutlass still hanging from his waist
still ready to cut his way through rainforest.

About the contributor

Born in Georgetown, Guyana, Grace Nichols is the author of many collections of poetry as well as one novel. She has received many honours for her work; they include the Commonwealth Poetry Prize (1983), the Guyana Poetry Prize (1996), and the Queen's Gold Medal for Poetry (2021).

Printed in Great Britain
by Amazon

26082471R00106